HISTORY:

OF QUIET BIRDS

December 4, 1990: Illinois Arts Council Award For Playwriting

April 10, 1993: Women's Theater Alliance – Impulse Studio Theater. (Informal Reading) – Chicago

June 21, 1993: Christian –In- Theater Arts (Cita) Playwriting Contest - Trinity Western University - (Finalist) British Columbia

September 24, 1993: Deep South Writer's Conference – James H. Wilson Full-Length Playwriting Award – First Prize – Louisiana

October 10, 1993: Studio Z – (Reading) – Chicago, Illinois

March 28, 1994: Playwright Preview Production – Urban Stages – (Reading) New York, New York

June 28, 1994: Theater On The Lake – Premiere Production Chicago - 6/28/94 - 7/02/94 - Chicago

July 29, 1994: Rising Star Community Theater –Jones Memorial— Community Center -- (Performance) 7/29/1994 – 7/30/1994 – Chicago Heights, Illinois

March 17, 2016: Austin Town Hall—Chicago Park District – March 17, 2016 – March 19, 2016 (Performance) Chicago, Illinois

AWARDS:
OF QUIET BIRDS

Individual Artist Playwriting Fellowship Award
Illinois Arts Council. 1993.

First Prize - James H Wilson Full Length Playwriting Award,
Deep South Writers Conference
University of Southwest Louisiana. 1993.

OF QUIET BIRDS

A PLAY IN THREE ACTS

Loretta A. Hawkins

ISBN-13: 978 – 0692915400
ISBN-10: 0692915400

This play is dedicated to the loving memory of my mother, Laurine (Blink) Hines Sanders, who taught me how to write, a gift for which I am forever grateful.

The World Premiere of *OF QUIET BIRDS* was produced by

The Chicago Park District
E. Wayne Worley, Artistic Director
Cynthia Jahraus, Assistant Artistic Director

OF QUIET BIRDS received its world premiere at Theatre on the Lake in Chicago, Illinois on June 28, 1994. It was produced by The Chicago Park District. (E. Wayne Worley, Artistic Director; Cynthia Jahraus, Assistant Artistic Director) It was directed by Dionne Hawkins; the costumes design was by Jana Stauffer; the sound design was Klaus Schuller; the production stage manager was Robin Hawkins; the assistant stage manager was Jackie Smith. The cast was as follows:

DAVID LEE TURNER	Joe Thompson, Jr
MARGRIT TURNER	Barbara Green
FRANKLIN TURNER	Renardo Bell
CORA LEE TURNER	Gina Taliaferro
THERESA BROWSER	Stephany McCullun
TYREE CARTER	Maurice Mitchell
JONATHAN LEE TURNER	Sanford Brantley
REVEREND WILLIAMS	Gregory Golden
MRS. BLACKWELL	Dionne Hawkins
TELEVISION ANNOUNCER	Klaus Schuller

ACKNOWLEDGMENTS

Mary Frye is the author of the poem used as the eulogy in this drama. The characters in this drama are fictitious, (with the exception of Dr. Helena Hicks of Baltimore, Maryland, who along with fellow professors and students from Morgan State College, staged the first successful lunch-counter sit-in), and are not meant to depict, portray, or represent any real persons or group of people. All characters (with the exception of Dr. Hicks), incidents, and dialogues are products of the author's imagination and are not to be construed as real. Any other resemblance to actual events or persons, living or dead, is coincidental.

OF QUIET BIRDS

Published by FIREKEEPER ARTISTRY
Chicago, Illinois

The wolf also shall dwell with the lamb...
And a little child shall lead them.
Isaiah 11:6

"When you awaken in the morning hush,
I am the swift, uplifting rush,
Of quiet birds in circled flight,
I am the soft star that shines at night."

Mary Frye
(1932)

CHARACTERS

FRANKLIN TURNER:
Forty-seven year old, head of the Turner family.

MARGRIT TURNER:
The forty-two year old wife of Franklin; a teacher.

JONATHAN L. TURNER:
Twenty-two year old son of the Turners, a law school student.

CORA LEE TURNER:
Seventeen year old daughter of the Turners.

DAVID LEE:
Youngest son of the Turners; age eight to twelve.

THERESA BROWSER:
Friend of CORA LEE, age seventeen.

REVEREND WILLIAMS:
Family pastor.

MRS. BLACKWELL:
Elderly neighbor.

SETTING

The year is 1955. The place is some town in North Carolina. The setting is the living room of the Turners and the small porch that leads to it. Although the living room is comfortable, it is a pretty room, edging on elegance. There are a few inexpensive painting on the walls, fresh flowers in vases and lace dollies on the arms of chairs as was the custom of that period. There are other artifacts to lend a touch of middle-class stability and a sense of well-being to the people that live here.

The porch is small, large enough to hold one or two people at most. It is situated so that the audience can see anyone who approaches the front door prior to their coming into the living room, which contains a sofa, chairs, end tables and a coffee table. Further back, stage left, is a large dining room table, complete with lace table cloth and a vase of flowers. At stage right, in the rear, there is an upright piano that is situated so the player's back is mostly to the audience when it is played. A television set is at stage right, front, facing the center of the stage so that when it is on, the audience can see its bluish glare, but not its picture. A center door leads to the other rooms.

The furnishings are of the style particular to the 1950s, U.S.A. It is a day in late May.

PROLOGUE

Slavery has ended almost a hundred years ago. The plan of the Unites States government to give each freed slave forty acres of land and a mule is a long ago broken promise. Most of those who had been slaves are dead now, but their narratives of misery, degradation, and horror lay latent in the minds and souls of those who came after. The memory of it keeps many blacks in check.

In the southern part of the United States, no one – black or white – even pretends that *anything* is equal, least of all the inalienable rights of life, liberty and the pursuit of happiness. Most blacks live in shacks, most whites do not. In many counties, white children ride to modern, well-equipped schools on heated busses while black children (those who are fortunate enough) walk long miles to run-down schools containing second-hand supplies. Those Blacks who do manage to become educated nevertheless, are frequently hired only for menial work.

This racial dichotomy is evident not only in housing, education and employment, but also has had almost a century to ferment unchallenged; it now permeates almost every common-day experience. Any black who is unwise enough to protest his lack of liberty, usually loses his life, with happiness being a thought not even worthy of contemplation.

In 1955, all over the South, blacks are oppressed, disenfranchised and segregated. They cannot eat in restaurants downtown or drink from public water fountains. They are barred from public toilets, parks, beaches, hotels, and many stores. In places where their money is welcomed (but they are not), provisions are made to keep the races separate; thus, blacks can sit only on the *back* of busses, in the *balconies* of movie houses, enter the *back* of many stores. The object is to ascertain that the races do not mingle, the implication being that whites are superior and blacks inferior.

Those blacks who carry within them the old memory realize that these conditions, though demeaning, are preferable to whips, chains, and mutilations, and so they persevere and acquiesce, and calmly and diligently teach their children how to survive this adverse environment.

Upon this scene, less than a decade earlier, had come, quietly and without fanfare, one of the most powerful technological forces of the twentieth century: television. Television allowed an entire nation to focus in on a single town, a single street, an individual. It allowed a nation to see, where before it could only imagine. It captured this scenario of sickness in the South, cut it open and laid its disease bare for all the world to see. But that came later. For now, it 'zaps' the minds, the imagination and the possibilities of the young. It causes conflict between those with the old memory and those who can now, at a glance, see the world; and with that new vision comes a new discontentment, an alien disquietude and a David and Goliath sense of hope and determination to, once and for all, put the ancient monster to rest.

8

ACT I
SCENE 1

THE HOUSE LIGHTS GO OFF

(Once it is quiet, the audience hears finger exercises on a piano. It is obviously being played by someone who has had lessons for several years and plays well. The finger exercises continue for several minutes, then stop for a second or two. When the music resumes, it is a beautifully calming, soft Chopin-like melody. After two minutes of this music…. The CURTAIN rises on..)

DAVID LEE

(In the living room. He is the one playing the piano. He plays for another two minutes, then suddenly begins playing Scott Joplin's, "The Entertainer." He is obviously enjoying this "forbidden music" when MARGRIT appears at the outside door. When DAVID LEE hears her keys in the door, he swiftly returns to the Chopin-like piece.)

MARGRIT

(Enters) Hello David Lee.

DAVID LEE

(Pretending he has not heard her coming.) Oh, hi, mama.

MARGRIT

That's some mighty beautiful playing, David Lee. Just keep on practicing. *(Hangs purse in closet)* Did you do your homework?

DAVID LEE

Yes ma'am. I did that as soon as I came home.

MARGRIT

You sure are something. I thank God every day for having a son like you. Two sons like you for that matter. I can't wait until your brother, Jonathan, comes home from school next week. He'll be surprised to see you so big and fine. *(She goes over, kisses him.)*

DAVID LEE

I can't wait, either.

MARGRIT

I guess I better go on in this kitchen and see about supper, then think about grading some of these papers. Notice I said, "Think about." *(Starts for the kitchen, then stops, listening.)* Where's Cora Lee?

DAVID LEE

She's not home yet.

MARGRIT

(Immediately upset) Not home yet? From school? Why it's five-fifteen already. Did she come home, and go back out? *(There is alarm in her voice)*

DAVID LEE

I don't think so. I came straight home from school and I haven't seen her.

MARGRIT

(Looking out window) That's not like your sister to be this late. Something must have happened.

DAVID LEE

Maybe she went to the library, Mama.

MARGRIT

She wouldn't do that without telling me. She knows how I worry.

DAVID LEE

She could've just run by there to get a book or something.

MARGRIT

It wouldn't take this long to get a book. *(She goes to the door, opens it and stands looking out for a few minutes. Presently she closes the door, paces the room.)* She doesn't need to be out late in times like these. Too much is going on.

DAVID LEE

(Continues to play softly until she closes the door, then moves away from the piano) What's going on?

MARGRIT

All this new talk of militancy. Just making white folks mad.

DAVID LEE

You mean they're *just* getting mad?

MARGRIT

(MARGRIT looks at DAVID, surprised by his observation) David Lee, go back and finish practicing.

DAVID LEE

I finished. *(Pauses)* Mama, can I watch television?

MARGRIT

May I.

DAVID LEE

I mean, may I watch television?

MARGRIT

(Distractedly) You have to do your homework first.

DAVID LEE

I did it, Mama, I told you already.

MARGRIT

(Still distracted) All right. Go on. *(Pauses)* David Lee, I think you're right. I'm going to the library to see if Cora Lee is there. That's the *only* place I can think she'd be at this time of evening. *(Gets her purse from closet)* Your father is going to be late tonight. He had to go see Dr. Robinson. You stay in the house, and if Cora Lee comes home, tell her I said stay in the house, too. Hear? *(David Lee is sitting crossed-legged in front of the television, engrossed, and does not answer)*

MARGRIT

Boy? Did you hear me?

DAVID LEE

(Distracted) Oh, yes ma'am.

MARGRIT

What did I say? Repeat it.

DAVID LEE

Stay in the house, and when Cora Lee comes home, tell her to stay in the house, too.

MARGRIT

O.K. I'll be back soon. Come lock the door, now. *(MARGRIT exits. DAVID LEE gets up, locks the door. He meanders to the piano, plays a little of "The Entertainer." He goes to the sofa, jumps up and down a few times on the cushions, and then dances back to the television. He flops on the floor in front of the television.)*

FRANKLIN
(Enters. He is a large, booming-voiced man whose speech is that of an uneducated laborer, which is what he is.) Hey, champ! What's going on? *(FRANKLIN throws his cap on the sofa and throws up his fists, feinting boxing. DAVID LEE runs to him with his fists up and they proceed to play box each other. It is a ritual with them.)* Whoa! Look at the champ! He's in top form, ladies and gentlemen! He's rushing the challenger. He throw a right to the head, a left to the chest. He's a force, ladies and gentlemen, a true force! The challenger back away. He don't have no kind of chance. He can't overpower the force of the champion. *(He laughs and hugs DAVID LEE, who then goes back to the television set. FRANKLIN hangs his cap in the closet.)* Boy, you wear me out. Where your mama?

DAVID LEE
She went to the library to pick up Cora Lee. She said she'll be right back. You hungry, too?

FRANKLIN
A little. *(FRANKLIN picks up a newspaper, sits on the sofa and begins to read. It is quiet for a while—son watching television— father reading newspapers.)*

CORA LEE
(Appears at the side door, unlocks it. ENTERS. She looks guilty as she hangs her purse in closet, put her books away.) Hi, Daddy. Hi, David Lee. *(DAVID LEE gives her a half-wave, without turning around. FRANKLIN peers over the top of the paper he is reading.)*

FRANKLIN

Well, Hello, Miss Princess. You must of just missed your mama.

CORA LEE

(Heading for kitchen.) What? I'll be right back. I've got to heat up the food.

FRANKLIN

David Lee said she went to the library to pick you up. You must of just missed her.

CORA LEE

(Enters from kitchen.) Oh. *(Pauses.)* Daddy, can I talk to you about something?

FRANKLIN

(Putting the paper down) Why sure, Miss Princess. You know you can always talk to me.

CORA LEE

(Hesitantly) Daddy, do you think colored folks ought to do something about our rights?

FRANKLIN

(He is suddenly too serious, too fast.) Do something like *what*, Cora lee?

CORA LEE

Like fight for them, Daddy. Like demand our rights. *(He stares at her coldly, unnerving her)* I don't know – do *something*!

FRANKLIN

I thought your Mama and me had explained this thang to you before. Cora Lee, I thought you understood.

CORA LEE

I *do*, Daddy.

FRANKLIN

I hope you're not listening to any fool people from the North coming down here making trouble. They don't know *nothing* about the South. They're just coming down here, getting they picture in the newspapers, then going on back up the road.

CORA LEE

I'm listening to somebody from down here, Daddy.

FRANKLIN

(Ignoring her) But we got to live here, Cora Lee, and if we make the wrong moves, we'll end up in the newspapers our own selfs – in the obituary section! *(Angrily)* Huh, we can't fight for our rights, girl. We don't have no rights.

CORA LEE

(Hesitantly) We *have* rights, it's just that we're being denied them. *(Pauses)* Who says we don't *have* rights?

FRANKLIN

(Angrily) The law says we don't have no rights, that's who. The white folks who own this town say it. The books say it. I say it. We don't have no rights. None!

DAVID LEE

If Daddy says it, it's true.

CORA LEE

(Covered by his explosion, but unwilling to back off) Then don't you think we ought to do something about it? Make them change the laws?

15

FRANKLIN
(Controlling himself) How, Cora Lee? How do we do something about it? How do we *make* them change the laws?

CORA LEE
Daddy, you heard about Dr. Helena Hicks? She was in the newspaper a few months back. She's that college professor at Morgan State that led a sit-in demonstration at a lunch counter in Baltimore, Maryland.

FRANK.LIN
Yeah, I heard bout her. She that woman going round telling colored folks to break the laws. Somebody need to see bout that woman. A whole lot of colored people is going to get hurt listening to that woman.

CORA LEE
But, Daddy, you have to listen to what she's saying. Have you really listened to her?

FRANKLIN
(Cynically) What's she saying, Cora Lee?

CORA LEE
She says one way to change the laws, in our situation, is to disobey them.

FRANKLIN
(Sarcastically) That makes a whole mess of sense, Cora Lee. Now, why didn't I think of that?

CORA LEE
Dr. Hicks held a sit-in. She and some of the students from her university walked right into that drug store, Daddy, sat down at that

lunch counter and placed an order. They refused to serve them, of course. So, they just sat there.

FRANKLIN
That don't make no kind of sense.

CORA LEE
But, it worked, Daddy. It worked!

FRANKLIN
I don't see how.

CORA LEE
That drug store chain started losing lots of money.

FRANKLIN
They don't care bout losing no money.

CORA LEE
But, they do, Daddy. The owner of the chain says that from now on all customers can sit at the lunch counter.

FRANKLIN
That's just one lil store.

CORA LEE
It's a whole chain of stores in Baltimore, Daddy.

FRANKLIN
Then, it's a few lil stores in one lil city. That ain't the rules of this whole country.

CORA LEE
But if we can win with the drug store chains, Daddy, Dr. Hicks says we can do the same thing with other businesses.

17

DAVID LEE
It's getting *real* late. *(Goes to window to look out for MARGRIT)*

FRANKLIN
This Dr. Hicks woman sounds like a dreamer to me.

CORA LEE
(Going on excitedly) Just think of all the places downtown that treats us so badly, Daddy. We can put them out of business, one-by-one until they start to treat us equal to white folks. *(She is overcome with the concept.)* Just think of the power of the sit-ins and boycotts.

DAVID LEE
(His curiosity has been piqued.) What's a sit-in? And, what's a boycott?

CORA LEE
Actually, they are opposite strategies. A sit-in is when a group of people deliberately go to a place they are not allowed to and they refuse to leave. And, a boycott is not going to a place until laws are changed.

DAVID LEE
Then, we don't have to worry about boycotting Fun-Town, do we? We can't go there already. *(Goes back to sprawl in front of television)*

CORA LEE
If it's a place we can't go because of our color, Dr. Hicks says we must deliberately break the law and go there.

FRANKLIN

Then, what do you do when the police come and deliberately arrest you?

CORA LEE

(Quietly) You go to jail.

FRANKLIN

Just like that, huh?

DAVID LEE

(Turning from television) What're we having for supper?

CORA LEE

(To DAVID LEE) The food is heating up, David Lee. We'll eat when Mama comes back. *(To FRANKIN)* Dr. Hicks says that if a law is unjust, Daddy, we *have* to break it, then accept the punishment. *(FRANKLIN gives her a cynical look.)* Don't you *see*? That way you can see how unfair the law is.

FRANKLIN

Well, this ain't in no Baltimore, Miss Princess, and I don't need to break no laws to see they ain't fair. You think I can't see that it ain't fair that I can't use a public toilet when I have to? Or, I can't get a drink of water from a fountain when I'm thirsty. You think I can't see it's unfair that I can't buy a sandwich and sit down and eat it in a restaurant when I'm hungry? Hell, I was born in this country! But, I have to stand on a bus so that no white person have to. And that white person got on after me, and we paid the same fare. You think I can't see all that ain't fair, Cora Lee? *(He goes to window, looks out as he continues to talk.)* I can't vote, can't go to a park, can't go to a beach, can't go to a public swimming pool. And, I pay the same taxes as the white man? *(He stops talking for a moment and turns from the window. When he begins talking*

19

again, his voice has taken on a gentler tone. He walks over to CORA LEE, looks deeply into her eyes and says softly) The longest day I live, I won't never forget the day your brother, Jonathan saw that amusement park for the first time. Your mama was pregnant with you and Jonathan was just a little bitty ol' thang. I was taking him with me out to the quarry that day and when we come close to that amusement park... what you call it?---

CORA LEE

Fun-Town.

FRANKLIN

Yeah, Fun-Town. We come close to that place and his little eyes lit up like a thousand June bugs was flying in em'. He looked in there and seen all them people walking round having fun, with that carnival music and bright lights and he started jumping up and down in the car like he done fell in a mess of hornets. "Let's go in there, Daddy!" he say, and I say, "We can't, son." He say, "Why can't we, Daddy?" I looked over at him and seen them eyes all lit up, so I lied and told him I didn't have no money. Told him we'd have to wait till payday. *(He pauses)* Well, after that, he kept after me to take him. All the time asking, "Is it payday? Is it payday, Daddy?" I felt bad lying to that boy so much, so one day I just up and told him the truth when he asked. After that, he never mentioned that place to me no more. Never did. *(He is quiet for a minute. Goes to look out window again. We come to realize that this window-looking is an unconscious habit, developed from years of being protective of his family. He turns from the window.)* After that, I usta drive thirty miles outa my way to keep from passing that amusement park when he was with me. *(Pauses)* I've been seeing injustice all my life, Cora Lee, just like you've been seeing it. I've been living with it so long that I don't just see it no more; I smell it, I hear it, I feel it every day oozing like pus from the pores of this town, like some sick-something disease there ain't no cure for. Now here I stand, being told by my daughter that I'm supposed to go out and break them laws and get my behind slung in jail, so that I can *see* that they ain't fair. Like I can't see that already.

DAVID LEE
What's taking Mama so long? I'm hungry.

CORA LEE
But Daddy, breaking the laws not to make *you* see. It's to make the world see. To make the world see that the laws are unfair.

FRANKLIN
You think the world give a damn bout us?

CORA LEE
Yes, Daddy. I think it does – but we have to try to fight back ourselves.

FRANKLIN
(He takes her hand, tries to reason with her) Miss Princess, a long time ago, our people did try to fight back. But it wasn't no use. They had the guns, they had the laws, they had the power. There wasn't nothing we could do.

CORA LEE
I know, Daddy.

FRANKLIN
We'd fight back and they'd kill us. Always with the law on they side. Always. So, finally we stopped fighting back. But, the killings went on. They had castrations, tar-and-feathers, drownings, and lynchings. It was a time when any white man could kill any colored

man, for any reason, and the law would just wink its eye and turn
its head.

CORA LEE
(Sympathetically) I know, Daddy.

FRANKLIN
(Depressed, deep in thought) Finally, the genocide, --- *(He looks
up with a sad smile.)* I learned that fancy word from your mama –
slacked off. By then, we had learned to get by.

CORA LEE
Sounds like plain old giving-in to me.

DAVID LEE
Daddy, can I fix me a sandwich?

FRANKLIN
Wait till your mama get back. *(To CORA LEE)* Look at the
Indians! The Indians was just about wiped off the face of this earth
because they kept fighting back. Who we supposed to fight
anyway, Cora Lee? The police force? Fight the whole damn army?
Go to war against the United States, you think? Why I'd be willing
to bet...

MARGRIT
(Enters. To CORA LEE) Where were you, Cora Lee? I went to the
library and Mrs. Whitmore said she hadn't seen you.

DAVID LEE
What took you so long, Mama? Can I make a bologna sandwich?

CORA LEE
I wasn't at the library.

MARGRIT

(To DAVID LEE) No! *(To CORA LEE)* I know that now, Cora Lee. Where were you?

DAVID LEE

Can I make a peanut butter sandwich, Mama?

CORA LEE

(Evasively) I had to go somewhere.

MARGRIT

(To DAVID LEE) No! *(To CORA LEE)* Go where?

DAVID LEE

Can I make a jelly sandwich?

MARGRIT

No!

DAVID LEE

Can I make a bread sandwich?

MARGRIT

(Distracted, waving him away) Make any kind of sandwich you want, David Lee, just stop interrupting! *(When MARGRIT says this, DAVID LEE, standing behind her reacts. His whole body perks up, his eyes light up and he dashes from the room. To CORA LEE)* Now, where did you have to go?

CORA LEE

To a meeting.

MARGRIT

(Puzzled) A meeting? A school meeting?

CORA LEE
No, but some students were there.

MARGRIT
Where? What kind of meeting was this?

(DAVID LEE enters, arms laden with peanut butter, jelly, mayonnaise, lunch meats, lettuce, tomatoes, and several kinds of breads. He goes to dining room table and proceeds to make a tall, messy sandwich. He is unnoticed by the others.)

CORA LEE
A meeting at Tyree Carter's house.

MARGRIT
Tyree? Why Tyree's a college student. Was it a meeting about college?

CORA LEE
No, Mama. It was… it was a meeting about Negroes getting our rights.

MARGRIT
(Shocked) What! What are you talking about, girl?

CORA LEE
It was just a meeting that the college kids started. We discussed what we could do to get rights for colored people in this town, that's all.

MARGRIT
(Upset) How could you go out of here, endanger *our* lives, and speak so calmly of it, Cora Lee? How could you?

CORA LEE

But we aren't thinking about violence, Mama. We're talking about *non-violent* resistance. Peaceful civil disobedience.

MARGRIT

(Incredulously) Non-violent resistance? Peaceful civ… Girl, what are you talking about?

CORA LEE

Strategies, Mama! Those are the strategies for the revolution.

FRANKLIN

(Booming) REVOLUTION! What in the HELL are you talking about! *(Notices DAVID LEE)* And what in the hell is that mess over there?

MARGRIT

David Lee! What are you doing? All that food!

DAVID LEE

You said I could make any kind of sandwich I wanted. I'm making a Dagwood sandwich.

MARGRIT

Boy, put that food back in the refrigerator. *(MARGRIT proceeds to help DAVID LEE carry food back to the kitchen.)*

CORA LEE

Revolution just means change, Daddy. That's all. It's time to change this town.

FRANKLIN

White folks hear you talking about some revolution, they got strategies, too. Lynching and bombings and sniping us with a shotgun from the back of a pickup truck. *(He goes over to her, stares her in the eye.)* You ever hear of a white person being arrested for killing a colored person in this town?

CORA LEE

No, sir.

FRANKLIN

How many kids at that meeting?

CORA LEE

About fifteen, sixteen counting myself.

FRANKLIN

That mean they could kill all sixteen of y'all and you know what would happen?

CORA LEE

No, sir.

FRANKLIN

Nothing. Nothing at all. Except we'd have sixteen funerals that week, that's all. You stay out of that mess! You hear?

CORA LEE

It's too late now, Daddy. We all pledged our commitment to this cause.

FRANKLIN

Then, that's too bad.

CORA LEE

But, I'm already in it, Daddy.

FRANKLIN
You just think you in it. *(MARGARIT enters)*

CORA LEE
But, tomorrow's the last meeting before our first protest. The *last* meeting!

(FRANKLIN and MARGRIT speak simultaneously)

FRANKLIN
AND YOU AIN'T GOING!

MARGRIT
AND YOU'RE NOT GOING!

CURTAIN

ACT I
SCENE 2

Time: Two days later, late Saturday morning.
Place: The Turners' living room.

(Before the curtains open, we hear piano playing. The CURTAIN rises on DAVID LEE, playing exquisitely beautiful music. CORA LEE enters from rear door, carrying fresh flowers, which she places in a vase on the dining room table after dancing with the flowers around the room. DAVID LEE continues to play.)

CORA LEE
Play, Orpheus!

DAVID LEE
(Correcting her) David Lee.

CORA LEE
I know, bird-brains. A person can pretend if they want to. **(Dancing around the room, again)** Oh, David Lee! I feel so... so alive! So new! So... so something! *(Hugs herself in this vivacious mood. Goes to DAVID LEE at the piano, sits and speaks to him passionately while he continues to play)* Have you ever felt so alive you didn't know what to do?

DAVID LEE
(Smugly) Nope, I always know what to do.

CORA LEE
(Enraptured by music, swaying.) Oh, David Lee. You are Orpheus. You are. Orpheus reincarnated.

DAVID LEE

Re – in –car- what? Is that his last name?

CORA LEE

No, dum-dum. Reincarnate is a word. *(Begins dancing again)* It means to come back to life. After you die, of course. Why, some folks believe that the soul of a living thing never dies. Only the mortal body dies. The soul lives on and on and on and on. Forever! I think so, too. Inside a different body, of course. *(Stops dancing near DAVID LEE)*

DAVID LEE

A different body!

CORA LEE

(Sitting beside him on piano bench.) Sure, let's supposed you died.

DAVID LEE

(Stops playing abruptly, turns to CORA LEE) Don't be supposing *me* dead!

CORA LEE

Just *suppose*, David Lee. If you died, this little puny body of yours would be gone. But you might come back as a.. a peacock. But you wouldn't be able to give the world your beautiful music as a peacock, would you? But you *could* spread out your magnificent, blue, and purple, and green iridescent feathers in all their glory for all the world to see and admire. *(She spreads her arms to demonstrate a peacock wings.)* And that would be the same thing, see? That would be the beauty that you would give to the world. But it would really be you – your soul – inside that peacock!

DAVID LEE
(Astonished) I would be a peacock?!

CORA LEE
If you were reincarnated. You could be anything.

DAVID LEE
I don't want to be no peacock. They're silly looking.

CORA LEE
So are you. Anyway, you're already been reincarnated, at least once, boy. Once upon a time, you use to be Orpheus, the magnificent musician. Now, you're David Lee Turner, silly looking little colored boy. We've got you now. *(She EXITS. Dancing.)* See you later, Orpheus.

DAVID LEE
(Calling after her, angrily) I'm not no Orpheus and I'm not going to be no peacock, either. *(Plays piano)* I'm going to be a lion. *(Roars like a lion. The doorbell rings, DAVID LEE goes to answer it, roaring and clawing the air.)*

THERESA
(Entering) Hi, David Lee.

DAVID LEE
(Roaring and clawing the air) Roar! Roar!

THERESA
(Calmly) What's your problem? *(DAVID LEE ignores her, goes to television, still roaring.)*

CORA LEE
(ENTERS. Hugs THERESA.) I'm so glad to see you, Tee. Girl, I got three new pairs of shoes to take to school. You've got to see them. I'll get them. *(EXITS to bedroom)*

THERESA
Three pairs! Wow! You're going to be really cool. *(Notices DAVID LEE at the television, still roaring.)* What's wrong with David Lee?

CORA LEE
(Off stage) He thinks he's a lion.

DAVID LEE
(To Theresa, angrily) I'm not going to be no peacock!

THERESA
I don't blame you.

DAVID LEE
I'm going to be a lion.

THERESA
Whatever makes you happy.

CORA LEE
(ENTER with three shoe boxes) Check them out, Tee.

THERESA
Wow! Black and white saddle oxfords. These are something else! Penny loafers! Here, let me put the pennies in them. Hey, blue suede! Out-of-sight! You're going to be stepping in style in college.

CORA LEE

(Turning serious) How was the meeting that I missed?

THERESA

Informative. The topic was "You-Will-Be-Scared." They said we have to try to internalize the fear, you know? Deal with it. They also said it's O.K. to be afraid.

CORA LEE

(After a long pause, quietly) Let's go.

THERESA

Aren't you going to tell anybody you're going?

CORA LEE

Are you crazy? If I told them, they wouldn't let me go! That's how I missed the last meeting, telling them. *(Pauses)* I know, I'll tell David Lee. *(Softly to DAVID LEE who is engrossed in television, roaring and clawing)* I'm going downtown, David Lee. Bye. *(CORA LEE and THERESA exit quickly. The closing door jars DAVID LEE from his world of make-believe. He turns from television momentarily.)*

DAVID LEE

(Quietly) Corrie?

FRANKLIN

(Enters, wearing pajamas, carrying newspapers) Who that just left?

DAVID LEE

Corrie and Tee, I guess.

FRANKLIN

Where they going this time of morning? It's not even noon, yet.

DAVID LEE

I dunno.

FRANKLIN

(Sitting on sofa, starting to read newspapers) What you watching, Champ?

DAVID LEE

The Cisco Kid. Want to watch it with me? Poncho's got them in trouble. Again.

FRANKLIN

Poncho's something else, ain't he? *(Puts newspapers down, lies on sofa, watching television)* Let's see what kind of mess that rascal get them into this time.

DAVID LEE

Yeah! *(The lights dim in such a manner to indicate the passage of hours. When the lights come back up, DAVID LEE is still watching television. FRANKLIN is asleep on sofa. MARGRIT ENTERS from rear, wearing an apron over her street clothes. She goes to sofa, shakes FRANKLIN.)*

MARGRIT

(Shaking him gently) Franklin, wake up honey. It's time to eat.

DAVID LEE

Yeah! I'm starving!

FRANKLIN

Huh. What? I musta fell asleep.

MARGRIT

Must have? Where's Cora Lee?

FRANKLIN

I thought *you* told her to go someplace. She been gone all day.

MARGRIT

(Alarmed) What! I was grocery shopping this morning, then I went by to visit Jackie Mae. Where did she say she was going?

FRANKLIN

I didn't see her. She was gone when I got up. *(To DAVID LEE)* Where did Cora Lee say she was going, boy?

DAVID LEE

I don't know.

MARGRIT

Did you see her?

DAVID LEE

Yes, ma'am.

MARGRIT

Well, what did she say?

DAVID LEE

(With indignation) She said I was going to be a peacock when I died. I told her I wasn't going to be no peacock nothing.

MARGRIT

David Lee, stop talking nonsense. I'm talking about did she say anything about where she was going. And I keep telling you to stop using those double negatives like that. Don't say no peacock nothing.

DAVID LEE

Yes, ma'am.

MARGRIT

(To FRANKLIN) I'm getting worried about that girl, Franklin. Something's happening to her.

FRANKLIN

She's just growing up, Margrit.

MARGRIT

No, it's something else. Like not telling us she had been attending those meetings at Tyree Carter's house. Cora Lee never used to lie to us.

FRANKLIN

Now, Margrit. The girl didn't exactly lie to us. She never said she was at the library.

MARGRIT

But, she implied she was there all those evenings she was late coming home. A lie of omission is still a lie. And, don't try to defend her when she's wrong, Franklin. That's why she's so spoiled now. You always let her have her way.

FRANKLIN

Good thang a lie ain't a rattlesnake. You'd be falling over dead about right now.

MARGRIT

Oh, so now I'm lying. I'm lying when I say you spoil her, huh? Well, what about last week when she wanted three new pairs of shoes to go away to college?

FRANKLIN

A person need shoes.

MARGRIT

Nobody needs *three* new pairs of shoes. And what about…
(The entrance door opens and CORA LEE ENTERS, slams door behind her and leans her back against it. Her hair and clothes are in a state of dishevelment. She is breathing heavily as though she has been running. FRANKLIN, MARGRIT and DAVID LEE stare at her.)

FRANKLIN

Where in hell have you been?

MARGRIT

(Softly) What happened to you, girl?

DAVID LEE

Corrie!

CORA LEE

I went downtown with some other students. *(She pauses)* The lunch counter sit-in was today. The first one in this town.

DAVID LEE

(Knowing the trouble to come. Dejected) Oh, boy. *(DAVID LEE turns to the television, ignoring the others)*

MARGRIT

(Shocked) What? A sit-in! You weren't part of it, were you? You're not a law-breaker!

FRANKLIN

(Simultaneously) Damnit! We told you not to go to that thang.

MARGRIT

See what I mean? She's just acting grown because you let her do what she wants to.

FRANKLIN

I told her not to go! *(To MARGRIT)* Don't start no mess with me, woman.

MARGRIT

We were worried to death about you! We didn't even know where you were.

CORA LEE

I told David Lee where I was going.

DAVID LEE

You didn't tell me nothing. *(Turning from television)* Y'all too loud over there. I can't even hear the television.

FRANKLIN

Turn that damn thang off.

DAVID LEE

(Turning off television) Aw, Daddy.

MARGRIT

(Turning CORA LEE's head to the side, inspecting her chin) You're bleeding! David Lee run and get the first-aid kit and a hot washcloth. *(DAVID LEE EXITS)*

CORA LEE

It's nothing, Mama. Just a little scratch.

FRANKLIN

(To CORA LEE.) What happened? *(DAVID LEE ENTERS with antiseptics, bandages and washcloth. MARGRIT proceeds to care for CORA LEE's wounds.)*

CORA LEE

It was horrible. Horrible! **(She goes to a chair, sits on the arm.)** There were three groups of us, five in each group. Our plan was to have the first group go in, Darryl, Tyree and them, and sit at the lunch counter. As soon as the police arrested the first group, then my group was going to go in. We'd sit down, get arrested, then the last group would go in.

FRANKLIN

Sounds crazy to me.

CORA LEE

(Her composure begins to break) But, but... *(She breaks into tears)* Mama, they beat them! They beat them over the head with clubs just for sitting at a lunch counter! *(She cries throughout)* Blood was everywhere. But Darryl, Tyree and them didn't run. Our group was outside on the sidewalk and we could see through the big display windows. *(She is re-living the event.)* A sensation came over me that I was watching a surreal movie, because it seemed too horrible to be true. Inside the store, one of the policemen hit at Ty with a .. a club, but Ty ducked. The billy club hit the lunch counter and broke in half. The police turned red, red, and then he hit Ty in the mouth with his fist. As hard as he could, Mama! He must have knocked out Ty's teeth because all you could see was blood pouring from Ty's mouth. The policeman's hand was dripping red with blood. The white people outside with us was screaming, "Kill the nigger! Kill the nigger."

FRANKLIN

You had no business being there!

CORA LEE

(She holds her right hand out, imitating the policeman) Inside, the policeman turned and looked at his hand like he was surprised to see blood on it. That seemed to make him madder. He threw Ty

on the floor and started kicking him in the stomach. I was scared. I was so scared. *(She allows herself to cry for a few seconds.)*

DAVID LEE
(Sympathetically) Don't cry, Corrie.

CORA LEE
I wanted to run, Mama, but I couldn't. I was frozen, staring through that window. The only thing that saved them was that we had called the news station to report that the sit-in was going to happen, and the television cameras were there. Another policeman said to the one kicking Tyree, "Them cameras, Troy." Then I guess Troy remembered that he was supposed to be arresting Ty for sitting at the lunch counter, not beating him for it, so he started dragging him out to the paddy wagon. They probably would have killed Tyree right there at the lunch counter if those television news cameras hadn't been there, Mama! Anyway, another policeman was dragging Darryl out, feet-first. They went past us on the sidewalk and I could see Darryl's head bumping on the concrete. Darryl was trying to protect his head with his arms and hands, like this. *(She demonstrates)* Then Morris, the leader of our group said, "Come on. It's our turn."

MARGRIT
Oh, no!

CORA LEE
(She hangs her head, trying to relieve the tension) We started inside but some other police blocked the way and wouldn't let us pass inside. We tried to push our way to the door, but the white people started pushing us back. We couldn't even get close to the door, so our group and the third group never even got inside. *(She drops her head as though in shame. All the time she is relating this tale, her parents are registering shock and disbelief.)*

MARGRIT

(She clasps her hands and looks upward) Oh, thank God! Thank God you didn't get inside. They would've hurt you for sure if you'd sat at that lunch counter. *(Angrily to CORA LEE)* That lunch counter is for WHITE people, Cora Lee!

DAVID LEE

When are we going to eat?

CORA LEE

Why, Mama?

MARGRIT

Hush, David Lee.

FRANKLIN

(Angrily) You don't know a thang about it. If you did, you wouldn't of been there.

CORA LEE

(Quietly, to MARGRIT) We have to use our bodies to free our minds. *(Shouting)* All we have are our bodies!

FRANKLIN

The girl done gone crazy right in front of our faces! Crazy!

MAGRIT

Honey, you're confused. That's not the right way. You can't break the laws. If you break the laws, no one can protect you. You'll have no defense.

CORA LEE

(With emotion) If I don't break the laws, no one will protect me, Mama. *(She turns to FRANKLIN)* I have no defense anyway. Can't you both see that?

MARGRIT

Cora Lee, we know things aren't right. They have never been right for us, but they are getting better. Why, every day I see little signs that race relations are improving. And colored people are advancing. Little by little. Just think, Cora Lee. My grandparents were slaves, slaves – and here we are - - free and everything. And we're doing just fine, honey. Just fine. We get along with the white folk and they don't bother us. You can't expect everything to just change overnight. It takes time to change things.

CORA LEE

Why?

FRANKLIN

(Fed-up) I've had enough of this nonsense, Cora Lee. You're acting like you done lost your mind, girl. All these new militants are messing with your mind. These white folk'll think nothing of killing you, me, your mama, David Lee, and the dog. Nothing! You hear me?

CORA LEE

(Hesitantly) Then I guess—I guess they'll – just have to kill me.

FRANKLIN

She done gone crazy. *(Stalks angrily to the window, peers out.)*

CORA LEE

(To FRANKLIN) Look at me. *(FRANKLIN continues to look out the window)*

MARGIT
Cora Lee! Stop talking foolishness.

CORA LEE
(Louder) Look at me, Daddy. *(He is too angry to turn around. She screams)* Look at me!

(He turns slowly, looks at her)

MARGRIT
Girl, you're getting too womanish for me, screaming at grown folk like you're crazy.

DAVID LEE
(Meekly) The food's getting cold.

CORA LEE
Daddy, am I somebody?

FRANKLIN
(Forcefully) You don't need me to tell you, you somebody. You ought to know you somebody.

CORA LEE
(Screaming again, nearly out of control) I want to know, am I somebody?

DAVID LEE
I know I'm somebody.

MAGRIT
Cora Lee!

FRANKLIN

(Turning to speak to MARGRIT) I told you she done gone crazy! You just might as well stay home tomorrow and take her to the doctor. How could this happen to her and we didn't even see it coming?

CORA LEE

(Pleading) Daddy! I'm just trying to make you see. You've got to see! A person is the sum total of their experiences. If all of my experiences tell me I'm equivalent to a pile of – *(She searches for a word)* – dirt, then I'm just dirt. I'm not somebody, I'm dirt.

FRANKLIN

(Emphatically, staring CORA LEE in the eye) You ain't no dirt! We ain't never had no dirt in our family.

DAVID LEE

I know I'm not no dirt!

CORA LEE

You say I'm not dirt, but the law says I am. Folks don't want dirt on a park bench, so you don't put dirt on a park bench. Well, I can't sit on the park bench either. Just like dirt. Folks don't' want dirt in a restaurant, so you can't take it in a restaurant. Well, I can't go in a restaurant either, Daddy. Just like the dirt. Name me one right that I have in this town that dirt doesn't have. Just one!

DAVID LEE

Dirt can't eat.

FRANKLIN

(To MARGRIT) Call Dr. Robinson first thang tomorrow morning.

CORA LEE

Daddy, you don't understand what I'm trying to tell you.

FRANKLIN

Naw, Cora Lee, I don't. And, I ain't even trying to, cause what you're talking about done got too many niggers lynched around here. All I'm trying to do is – to – survive—these people. Just stay alive. And, if you want to keep on gulping down these white folks air, you better learn the same thang. All that education you getting gonna get you dead, girl.

CORA LEE

See! See! That's what I'm talking about. Now they own the air. How can white people own the air! How can anybody own the air! You're just giving in to them, Daddy.

FRANKLIN

They own the water, don't they? And, won't let us near it. They own all the land – they control that. If they could, they'd charge us for the air we breathe. Yeah, like a air tax. And we'd have to pay it, wouldn't we? They just ain't thought to tax us for the air – yet. *(Pauses, as if finalizing his decision)* Yeah, they own the air.

CORA LEE

Daddy, don't you see? They're crazy, not me? This hatred—this quest for power is insanity. Insane people are controlling us and we're just letting them!

FRANKLIN

Yeah, we letting them. We letting them control us and they letting us don't get lynched. That's the agreement.

CORA LEE

But, that's letting them have their way.

FRANKLIN

Then we letting them have they way.

MARGRIT

Cora Lee, we're just trying to get along with these white folks. And, we do. We get along fine. Just fine.

CORA LEE

(Going to MARGRIT) Yes, we get along with white folks, Mama. Because we let them treat us like dirt under their feet. It's easy to get along with white folks being dirt. All you have to do is just lay there and be dirt. And, if on a hot day, you get thirsty and can't drink out of the water fountain, all you have to do is remember you're dirt and dirt doesn't need water. Or, if you're away from home, Mama, and get hungry, but can't eat because all the restaurants won't serve colored, just say, oh, yeah, I forgot, I'm dirt! Dirt doesn't get hungry, or eat, as David Lee said. Dirt doesn't have any needs. But it doesn't have any rights, either! Last summer when I went to Chicago to stay with Aunt Pearl, I couldn't use the toilet at the train station because all of the toilets are for whites. I had to go out in the weeds behind the station like a dog. Well, next time, I can just act like dirt and remember that dirt doesn't need to pee and everything is actually improving in this great country of ours, anyway. Except that I'm tired of being treated like dirt! I'm a human being and I want to be treated like one. And, I don't want to wait! I want it now, Mama! Now!

MARGRIT

(To CORA LEE) Now, there you go screaming, again. What's *wrong* with you?

FRANKLIN

This is just suicide talk! Do you want to die? Answer me! Do you want to die?

CORA LEE

No, Daddy, I don't want to die. But… living here. It's like… It's like…

FRANKLIN

I don't care what it's like. If you don't want to die, stop talking this suicide talk! Stop it, hear? That fool Tyree's probably dead by now. And, you think, if he is, that anybody's going to pay for it? He colored, Cora Lee, so he'll just be dead.

CORA LEE

(With emotion, shouting) If he's dead, then I say good! Good! If he's dead, then he died like a *man*, with dignity, asserting his right to be treated like a human!

FRANKLIN

You think getting kicked in the teeth, getting lynched, getting killed is dignified? What's dignity, anyway? For us, there ain't nothing but survival. Stay alive! LIVE!

CORA LEE

(Crying) But, Daddy! How can I live? *(Pleading)* How can I live like this? *(Dropping to floor)* Tell me how can I live? *(Folding into herself)* I am not dirt. I – am – a- human – being! *(She is on the floor, head touching floor, moaning)* How can I live like this?

FRANKLIN

(He is standing above her, trying not to give in to his emotions) Don't do this. Don't do this to me, Cora Lee. *(He loses the battle for control. He drops to one knee, trying to cradle her)* Please, don't do this, baby. I don't want you to do this. I know what you're talking about, but ain't nothing we can do about it. Nothing!

DAVID LEE

(He has come over to the two of them. DAVID LEE throws his arms around CORA LEE in concern) Don't cry, Corrie. Don't cry.

MARGRIT

(Completes the circle, embracing them all. She drops to one knee, looks upward and seems to be actually calling) God! Help us! Please help us!

CURTAIN

ACT I
SCENE 3

Time: One week later
Place: The Turners' living room.

(First we hear the soft murmur of a vacuum cleaner going, then the sound of piano finger exercises. The CURTAIN rises on MARGRIT, CORA LEE, both of whom are cleaning up and DAVID LEE, who is practicing the piano. He is wearing a baseball uniform. CORA LEE is polishing furniture and MARGRIT is vacuuming. FRANKLIN is seated on the sofa, reading the newspapers. MARGRIT vacuums for a minute and then turns the vacuum off.)

DAVID LEE
(Plays for a minute, then stops and turns, speaking to MARGRIT.) May I go over to Jojo's house to play ball, Mama?

MARGRIT
If you're finished practicing the piano. *(Exits to rear, taking vacuum cleaner with her.)*

CORA LEE
Hey, you promised to play my favorite song.

DAVID LEE
Aw, Corrie, I'll play it when I come back. I gotta go practice for our game tomorrow afternoon.

CORA LEE
Oh, no! First of all, I probably won't be here when you get back. Second of all, what is a Saturday morning if a girl can't hear her favorite song played by her favorite little brother. *(She goes and hugs him from behind, leans over and kisses him on the cheek.*

48

He wipes her kiss away, knowing he's trapped.) And, third of all, aren't you the same exact person I gave my entire Archie Comic book collection to in exchange for one year of playing on request?

DAVID LEE
Aw, Corrie.

CORA LEE
'Aw, Corrie' nothing. I only ask you to play once a week while I'm house cleaning. You're not cheating me, boy. *(Starts to leave, stops, turns)* Start playing.

DAVID LEE
Aw, *(He turns to piano and begins playing the most exquisite melody imaginable. It is obvious that he has played this piece for her before. CORA LEE is completely mesmerized by the beautiful music.)*

CORA LEE
(Flinging her arms and dancing around the room.) Oh, David Lee, you are Orpheus. You are Orpheus and I am Eurydice. Your music is magical. You are Orpheus. You really are. *(She dances out of room toward bedroom.)* Keep playing, Orpheus – and I, Eurydice, will do an enchanting dance. *(Exits)*

DAVID LEE
(Continues playing for a few minutes) Who's Orpheus, anyway? *(Glances several times at FRANKLIN. Stops playing, goes over to FRANKLIN)* Daddy, do you…

CORA LEE
(Entering) Hey, Orpheus! What's the deal?

DAVID LEE
I just have to ask Daddy something. I'm going to finish.

CORA LEE

Promise?

DAVID LEE

I *promise. (CORA LEE EXITS)* Daddy?

FRANKLIN

(Still reading paper) Huh?

DAVID LEE

Know what Willie Tee told me yesterday, Daddy?

FRANKLIN

Unh-un.

DAVID LEE

He said the white folks are going to cut off the penis of all the colored people, stuff them in our mouths, then throw us in the Kalichooch River. *(Pauses)* Willie Tee said there won't be any more colored folks left in this town. *(Waits for a response from FRANKLIN)* Did you hear me?

FRANKLIN

I heard you.

DAVID LEE

Well?

FRANKLIN

(With newspaper still held in front of him. FRANKLIN turns to look at DAVID LEE) Well, what?

DAVID LEE

Well, what do you think?

FRANKLIN

I think Willie Tee ain't got good sense. That's what I think.

DAVID LEE

But, his daddy told him that.

FRANKLIN

His daddy the reason he ain't got good sense. His daddy ain't got none. First of all, half the colored folks in this town don't even have a penis.

DAVID LEE

(Shocked) They don't!

FRANKLIN

Nope.

DAVID LEE

They told you?

FRANKLIN

Naw, boy. Folks don't walk around talking 'bout what they got or don't got. Everybody know, anyway. Remember I talked to you 'bout the mens and the women? *(Coachingly)* You know.

DAVID LEE

Oh, you mean about women. Yeah, I know about women. *(Pause)* Oh, I see what you mean.

FRANKLIN

You ain't worried, is you? I mean 'bout Willie Tee running off at the mouth like that?

DAVID LEE

(Hesitantly) A little. *(Blurting out his secret fears)* I mean, I need my penis, Daddy. If they cut if off, what will I do when I have to use the bathroom?

FRANKLIN

That'll be the least of your worries.

DAVID LEE

Huh?

FRANKLIN

Look, boy. Don't believe everything that come out of Willie Tee's mouth. He ain't got good sense, his daddy ain't got none cause he idle-brained, and the two of them together couldn't figure out how to boil water. Now, I got to get on out of here. If I be late for my appointment with Dr. Robinson, Dr. Robinson's jaw get tighter than a vise. *(Getting ready to leave)* Now, I'll talk to you later about this. And, don't go worrying your mama none with this men's talk. O.K.?

DAVID LEE

O.K., Daddy.

FRANKLIN

(Going to rear door, calling to MARGRIT) I'm gone, sugar-sweets! I'll be back as soon as I leave Dr. Robinson's office.

MARGRIT

(From off stage) Bye, Honey! Be careful.

FRANKLIN

(To DAVID LEE) See you later alligator. *(EXITS)*

DAVID LEE

After while, crocodile. *(DAVID LEE returns to the piano and continues to play Cora Lee' favorite. He plays for a minute or two, then the doorbell rings)* I'll get it. *(Runs to answer the door. It is THERESA. He invites her in)* Hi, Tee!

MARGRIT

(Enters, carrying books and stack of papers. She goes to the table, begins grading papers) Why, hello Theresa. Come right on in, dear. I haven't seen you for weeks. How're your parents?

THERESA

Hello, Mrs. Turner. Hi, David Lee. They're fine, Mrs. Turner. Mama said to tell you hello. *(To DAVID LEE)* You play beautifully, David Lee.

DAVID LEE

(Not wanting to get back on the subject of piano playing. Hastily) Thanks. *(To MARGRIT)* I'm through practicing Mama. I'm leaving now.

MARGRIT

O.K. Son. Just be sure to come home early. Remember your big brother's coming home today.

DAVID LEE

(Running to piano, grabbing his baseball cap and ball) O.K., Mama. I'll remember. *(Exits Quickly)*

MARGRIT

(Proudly) Lord, that boy is going to be the death of me yet. He eats like a wolf and runs like there's no tomorrow. Didn't even say good-bye to you.

THERESA

Oh, that's alright, Mrs. Turner. At least he's not a lion. *(PAUSE)* Do you know if Corrie's ready yet?

MARGRIT

(Suspiciously) Ready? I don't know but I'll call her, Theresa. *(Goes to rear door, calls)* Cora Lee! Cora Lee! Theresa's here, dear. *(Returning to papers on table)* Well, where are you two off to?

THERESA

We're going downtown, Mrs. Turner
.

MARGRIT

(Unable to conceal her alarm) Oh! You girls going shopping or to the movies?

THERESA

Cora Lee didn't mention it? It might be better, Mrs. Turner, if Corrie…

CORA LEE

(Enters. She has changed into street clothes form her cleaning clothes) Hi, Tee! I'm ready.

MARGRIT

Cora Lee. You didn't mention to me that you were going out, dear.

CORA LEE

I'm going out.

MARGRIT

Well I know that now. Theresa just told me. Where are you girls off to?

CORA LEE

We're going downtown.

MARGRIT

I know that too Cora Lee. Where downtown?

CORA LEE

(Softly) We're going to a sit-in.

MARGRIT

(Softly) No.

CORA LEE

Mama...

MARGRIT

(Louder) No, Cora Lee.

CORA LEE

Mama, please. Don't...

MARGRIT

No, Cora Lee. You're not going. *(Softly)* You'll get hurt.

CORA LEE

(She is silent. When she does speak it is so softly that it is barely audible) I'm already hurt. I was born hurt.

MARGRIT

(Angrily) I'm not talking about hurt feelings, girl. I'm talking about serious, permanent damage. Something you might have to live with

the rest of your life. Like Dora Henderson. Messed up for life. *(Pleading)* I can't understand you, Cora Lee. You know they bombed the Henderson's house last week!

CORA LEE
That's why I have to go, Mama. This is 1955 and it's time we stopped this kind of craziness. Past time.

MARGRIT
Wasn't Dora's boy, Leo, part of that sit-in last week?

CORA LEE
Yes, Leo was there. And, he was so brave, Mama. You should have seen him when…

MARGRIT
Don't you understand Cora Lee? The bombing was retaliation against him for sitting-in. It was a warning!

THERESA
But, they've been bombing us ever since they discovered dynamite, Mrs. Turner.

CORA LEE
The Chinese discovered it, Tee. These folks just use it. On us. It probably replaced tar-and-feathering because it's not as messy to them.

MARGRIT
Poor Dora. Burns all over her face, arms and chest. By the time they drove her all the way to Mills County, her clothes had stuck to her burns. Jackie Mae said they almost *killed* her just trying to take her clothes off.

CORA LEE

(Angrily) And we have a hospital right here in this town.

MARGRIT

But, that's the white hospital, Cora Lee!

CORA LEE

(To Theresa) When we finish sitting in at the lunch counters, we'll have to…I guess, lay-in at the hospital in town. These people are crazy!

MARGRIT

Cora Lee, you act like these white people are different from white people in other places. If they were, we would have just moved a long time ago and solved all our problems.

CORA LEE

(Shocked) Mama, you think all white people are like these white people down here? These are *crazy* white people!

MARGRIT

(Calmly) They treat us like they do because they're white, Cora Lee. Not because they're crazy.

CORA LEE

(Incredulously) Mama! Mama! You're an educated woman. How can you even think such a thing? You're as prejudice as they are. They throw us all into one bag and say we're all the same because we're all the same color. And we call that prejudice! Well, that's what you're doing. You're saying they all are mean and evil just because they're white. That's just crazy!

MARGRIT

You're the one that's crazy, Cora Lee, because you're the one that will be getting killed. Not me.

CORA LEE

Then, they'll have to kill me, Mama, cause I'm going.

MARGRIT

I refuse to give you permission to go.

CORA LEE

(Sadly) Then, I go without your permission.

MARGRIT

(Exasperated) What are you trying to do? What are you trying to do, girl?

CORA LEE

I'm just trying to be free.

MARGRIT

(Softly, pleading) Cora Lee, they'll kill you. I can feel it.

CORA LEE

They're already killing me, Mama. *I* can feel it.

MARGRIT

I'm not going to just stand here and let you go to your death.

CORA LEE

(Exasperated) But, I've been just going to my death every day in this town. Every day. Don't you understand that?

MARGRIT

(Shouting) I'm not talking about the death of your spirit, girl, or your soul! I'm talking about DEAD DEAD. And one thing's for sure. Once you're dead, there is *no* hope.

CORA LEE
(Quietly) There is no hope now, Mama. Unless I do this.

MARGRIT
All our lives, your father and I have worked with only one goal in sight -- to give you children a good life and a chance. We put all our hope in you. *(Pauses)* Franklin's people and my people were sharecroppers, like almost all colored people around here were, some thirty years back. You know that. But, we struggled, Cora Lee, and tried to advance. We always felt that if we could just get the three of you through college, things would be so much better for you. Your brother, Jonathan, is the first somebody in either family to go to law school. *(She goes to CORA LEE, touches her face)* And, you, so smart. Graduating next week from high school in the top ten in your class. Scholarship to college. Your future is so bright, honey, it's like you're a shooting star. And, you're ready to throw it all away by getting arrested and going to jail? I just can't understand it, Cora Lee. I just can't understand!

CORA LEE
Mama, you're not...

MARGRIT
If you get arrested, these white folks won't *ever* let you get a job in this town. They won't even hire you to clean their houses!

CORA LEE
I have no intention of cleaning their houses, Mama. For as long as I can remember, colored folks been cleaning *white* folks houses. It's time they started learning how to keep their own houses clean. And, I *am* going.

MARGRIT
You aren't grown yet, young lady. You don't just *tell* me what you're going to do.

CORA LEE

I know that Mama.

MARGRIT

In this house, you still obey the first commandment: Honor thy father and mother.

CORA LEE

I do honor you, Mama. You know that.

MARGRIT

(Angrily) How do you honor me if you can't even obey me when I tell you right?

CORA LEE

(Frustrated. Shouting back) But, you're not telling me right, Mama! If I listen to you, I'll spend my whole life being treated like dirt.

MARGRIT

But, at least you'll live.

CORA LEE

I'd rather die fighting to assert my humanity than to live denying it.

MARGRIT

Fancy words, Cora Lee. Just fancy words. You always did have a way with words. But, they're just fancy, empty words.

CORA LEE

But, they're true, Mama!

MARGRIT

(Emphatically) Whether they are or aren't doesn't matter. I say stay here. -- You stay here.

CORA LEE

(To THERESA) Wait for me outside, Tee. *(THERESA exits)* Mama, have you ever known me to disobey you?

MARGRIT

No, not recently. But what you did at three let me know you were as stubborn as they come. Sticking your hand through the fence, eating up old Miss Mable's strawberries, next door. No matter how many times I spanked you, you went right back and ate some more. Finally, you got into a mess of green ones, and after they finished with you, I didn't have to say another word. You were so sick, to tell you the truth, *I* thought you were going to die.

CORA LEE

(Softly) Mama, do you know that I love you?

MARGRIT

Yes, I know you do.

CORA LEE

Mama, I love you and I respect you. I want you to be proud of me. But, I'm going to disobey you today. I'm going to this sit-in.

MARGRIT

No, you're not.

CORA LEE

Yes, I am. *(She steps around her mother and heads for the door. MARGRIT grabs her around the waist from behind)*

61

MARGRIT

Cora Lee, I'm begging you. I'm begging you, girl. *(CORA LEE stops struggling. She throws her head back onto her mother's shoulder, lets it rest there. CORA LEE is crying now.)*

CORA LEE

Mama, if I don't go, I won't ever be right. *(Suddenly she breaks free of her mother's grasps and rushes out of the door.)*

MARGRIT

(Calling) Cora Lee! Cora Lee! *(She slowly goes to the sofa, puts head on arm of sofa and cries. Suddenly she stands, paces floor, then goes to telephone, dials)* Hello! Connie, this is Margrit. Is Franklin still there? How long ago did he leave? Yes, something's wrong. There's going to be big trouble downtown. Big trouble! I'm so scared. Cora Lee and...

JONATHAN

(Enters living room, carrying suitcase) Mama, what's wrong!

MARGRIT

(Turns, sees JONATHAN, drops telephone, runs to JONATHAN, throws herself into his arms.) Oh Jonathan! Jonathan! Thank God you're home!

CURTAIN

ACT I
SCENE 4

Time: It is a few days later.
Place: The Turners' living room.
(Before the curtain rises, but after the lights dim, voices of FRANKLIN and DAVID LEE can be heard. The curtain rises on father and son in Turner living room, boxing)

FRANKLIN
(Holding out palm of hand for DAVID LEE to hit) Hit it! Hit it! Ladies and gentlemen, this fight's entering the tenth round. Although the challenger is still standing, the champion; the Brown Bomber, is stalking him and we can see the challenger done weakened.

MARGRIT
(Enter, carrying fresh flowers that she begins arranging in a vase) The challenger best sit his old self down.

FRANKLIN
Oh, the champion is closing in for the finish, ladies and gentlemen. He ain't showing no kind of mercy. The challenger is... *(Suddenly stops, stands completely still. Hand slowly goes to heart.)*

DAVID LEE
Something the matter, Daddy?

MARGRIT
(Starts to run to him, stops short) Are you O.K.?

FRANKLIN
(Collecting self) Sho am, sugar-sweets. I sho am. I just need to lay down a bit. *(MARGRIT comes to him, he puts his arm over her shoulder for support)*

63

MARGRIT
(Comfortingly) You just need to get more rest. *(To DAVID LEE
who is following behind them)* David Lee, I'll get him to bed. You
finish practicing your piano lessons. *(FRANKLIN and MARGRIT
EXIT)*

DAVID LEE
*(Falling back. He lingers by the piano, sits and begins playing.
The doorbell rings and he runs to answer it.)* Mom, it's Rev.
Williams! *(Turning away from the door)* Come in, Rev. Williams.
Have a seat.

REV. WILLIAMS
(Enters, but does not sit) Hello David Lee. Boy, that sure was some
fine-sounding music you were playing just now. Sounded like
something from heaven.

DAVID LEE
Thank you, sir.

REV. WILLIAMS
Yes, siree. It's about time you started playing a song or two for us
at the Morial Street Baptist Church on Sundays. I'll talk to Elder
Sanders about it.

MARGRIT
(Enters) Why, hello, Rev. Williams.

DAVID LEE
Excuse me, Mama. May I go over Jojo's house?

MARGRIT
Yes, but wait until I get the blackberry cobbler I fixed for his
mother. *(Exits)*

REV. WILLIAMS
(Sitting on sofa) Is Cora Lee home, David Lee?

DAVID LEE
No, sir. She and Jonathan went shopping for the party tomorrow.

REV. WILLIAMS
Oh, you're having a party?

DAVID LEE
Yes, sir. Daddy says they're having whiskey and some low-down music.

REV. WILLIAMS
Oh.

DAVID LEE
It's a graduation party for Cora Lee, but it's for Jonathan too. Him coming home from law school. Willie Tee said he wouldn't be no colored lawyer in the South. But, Daddy's proud Jonathan's going to be a lawyer.

REV. WILLIAMS
I am too.

MARGRIT
(Returning with a pie wrapped in a flowered dishcloth) Be sure to hold it with two hands now, so the juice won't spill.

DAVID LEE
I know.

MARGRIT
And, don't drop it.

DAVID LEE
I won't. I want to eat some. Bye, Mama. Bye, Rev. Williams.
(EXITS)

REV. WILLIAMS
I understand that Cora Lee's not here now?

MARGRIT
No, Rev. Williams. She went shopping with her brother. They should be back in a few minutes though.

REV. WILLIAMS
Is Franklin here? I would like this to be a family conference, if possible.

MARGRIT
He's here, Rev. Williams, but he's not feeling well. In fact, he's in bed. It's just as well. He gets so upset whenever we discuss this subject.

REV. WILLIAMS
You can't blame the man. Here he's worked all these years to raise decent, law-abiding children and then one out there just trying to get to jail. Any man would have difficulties with circumstances such as those, Margrit.

(We can hear CORA LEE and JONATHAN on the porch, before entering.)

JONATHAN
I just can't believe that nothing's changed around here. Everything's the same.

CORA LEE
This town has never been accused of being progressive, Jon.

(They both enter the living room, arms full of bags. They see minister and speak.)

JONATHAN
(Heartily) Hey! Rev. Williams.

CORA LEE
(Quietly) Hello, Rev. Williams.

JONATHAN
I'll be right back, sir. Let me empty my arms. *(JONATHAN and CORA LEE EXIT to rear.)*

REV. WILLIAMS
He sure is a mighty fine, young man, Margrit. You and Franklin have done yourself proud with him. Yes, you have.

MARGRIT
(Nervously) Rev. Williams, I know I asked you here to talk to Cora Lee, but don't be too hard on her. She's really not a bad person. You know that. She's just confused. She…

JONATHAN
(Entering with CORA LEE. JONATHAN goes to REV. WILLIAMS shakes hand and embraces.) It's certainly good to see you again, Rev. Williams. Why I was just thinking about you the other day.

REV. WILLIAMS
You were, were you? What were you thinking about, boy?

JONATHAN
Actually, it started off me thinking about Corrie and that Christmas play the church put on when she was in the -- what was it-- fifth grade. Remember? She was an angel and accidently fell off the

ladder? You were St. Gabriel and just happened to be standing underneath and caught her. She probably would have cracked her skull open if you hadn't been there.

REV. WILLIAMS
(Laughing) Well, what good is a saint if he can't catch a falling angel every now and then? You two were some mischievous little somethings back then, but you sure have matured into a fine, fine young man.

JONATHAN
Thank you, sir. *(REV. WILLIAMS, MARGRIT and JONATHAN all laugh, remembering the past. CORA LEE is conspicuous in her solemnity. REV. WILLIAMS notices her.)*

REV. WILLIAMS
(Clearing throat. To JONATHAN) Your mother asked me to come here to speak to Cora Lee. Get her back on the right track. Talk some sense into her.

JONATHAN
Well, sir, eh, I think I understand what Cora Lee is trying to do. Those tactics might not work, being outside of the law, but I understand what she's trying to do.

REV. WILLIAIMS
Oh, you do, do you? You understand getting arrested, going to jail, and creating a criminal record for yourself?

JONATHAN
Well, sir I-- well, yes, I understand the philosophy of civil disobedience and non-violent resistance. It's just that what Cora Lee is doing, is jeopardizing her future and taking a risk on her personal safety.

REV. WILLIAMS
(In agreement) That's what I'm trying to say.

JONATHAN
Well sir. I have to be running. I'm meeting some friends. Excuse me.

REV. WILLAIMS
You're excused, boy. Just keep studying hard. You'll make it.

JONATHAN
Thank you, sir. *(Kisses MARGRIT on the cheek)* Bye, Mom. *(Kisses CORA LEE guiltily)* Bye, Corrie. *(EXITS)*

REV. WILLIAMS
Yes, a fine young man. *(To CORA LEE)* Come sit down my child. We must talk. *(She sits)* Child, I'm here today to try to save not just your soul, but your body as well. These folks here will kill you faster than they crucified Jesus Christ. Cora Lee, all I'm asking you to do is follow the path of righteousness and you will be rewarded.

CORA LEE
How?

REV. WILLAIMS
Pardon me?

CORA LEE
How will I be rewarded, Rev. Williams?

REV. WILLIAMS
The kingdom of heaven will be yours.

CORA LEE
What about the kingdom of earth?

MARGRIT

Cora Lee!

REV. WILLIAMS

(To MARGRIT) It's alright, Margrit. I'm accustomed to dealing with the wayward of the world... *(To CORA LEE.)* Child, the kingdom of earth is promised to no man. All we're promised is the kingdom of heaven. And, that should suffice.

CORA LEE

Well, it doesn't. I don't want to wait until I die to be free. I want to be free now.

MARGRIT

You *are* free Cora Lee.

REV. WILLIAMS

It takes time for things to change, child. But, in the meanwhile, we can't just break laws.

CORA LEE

(Excited) Why not? They're unfair and they're based on race. Racist laws.

REV. WILLIAMS

This way of life is the Lords will. Ours is not to question why.

CORA LEE

That's why we're in the mess we're in now! And, I'm changing churches!

MARGRIT

Cora Lee, stop talking foolishness. Our family's been members of Morial Street Baptist Church ever since I can remember.

CORA LEE
I don't care. I don't need a leader with a slave mentality. Where can he lead me?

MARGRIT
Cora Lee! You're embarrassing me!

REV. WILLAIMS
Cora Lee, you've grown up in Morial Street Baptist Church. You were baptized there as a baby. You are a member of our junior choir. Was -- anyway, before you started trying to change the world and stopped coming to practice.

CORA LEE
So, I'm supposed to accept this mess, huh? Just act like I'm dirt?

REV. WILLIAMS
How do you think we feel, at the church, knowing you were arrested a few days ago for breaking the law?

CORA LEE
Jesus was arrested. They said he was breaking the law, too.

REV. WILLIAMS
(Impatiently) Girl, they turned trained dogs loose on those protesters yesterday. And those police were swinging those billy clubs like they were up at bat. And, you know whose heads were the balls. It's suicide! Suicide! I saw the whole thing on television. What you're doing is not safe!

CORA LEE
Nothing is safe and no place is safe.

MARGRIT

Home is safe! Church is safe! School is safe! You just leave those white folks alone. Stop trying to integrate with them!

CORA LEE

Integration has nothing to do with wanting to be with white people. Nothing. *(Suddenly someone is knocking on the door outside and calling CORA LEE.)*

THERESA

(From outside) Corrie! Hey, Corrie! *(Rushing in)* Corrie, Corrie, you've got to come. Now!

CORA LEE

Tee, what's the matter?

THERESA

They filled the jail downtown, so they're taking us to Mills County Jail. Tony told me to get as many people as I could so we can fill that jail, too! We've got two car loads of people outside, waiting. Come on!

CORA LEE

(Bolts from the room) Bye, Mama. I'll be back. *(The screen door slams behind her)*

THERESA

(Left standing there unexpectedly with the adults) Good evening, Mrs. Turner. Good evening Rev. Williams. How ya'll doing today? *(She remembers her mission)* I...I... bye! *(She bolts, the screen door slamming behind her)*

MARGRIT

(Running after CORA LEE in delayed reaction.) Cora Lee! Cora Lee! *(She exits, the screen door slams after her.)*

REV. WILLIAMS

Well! Do Jesus!

CURTAIN

ACT II
SCENE 1

Time: Two days later.
Place: The Turners' living room.

(The curtain opens on scene is the living room of the Turners, which is decorated for a party. There are banners and streamers, balloons and other party paraphernalia. Two large banners are hanging diagonally so that the audience can see both clearly. One says "Happy Graduation" and the other "Welcome Home." All members of the cast are present, except REV. WILLAIMS. There are friends and neighbors present, as well.

Before the curtain rises, we can hear the faint strains of rhythm and blues music. As the music gets louder, we hear talking and laughter and sounds of a party. As the CURTAIN rises, some couples are dancing to the music which is playing on a record player, while others on the sidelines encourage the dancers on.

The mood is festive, carefree and happy in contrast to previous scenes. The dancers dance the entire record, even DAVID LEE dances with a comical lady. There is much laughter. When the music stops, everyone cheers. FRANKLIN comes to the middle of the room and makes a toast.)

FRANKLIN
Yeah! Me and Margrit thank y'all for coming to help celebrate two big thangs with us. First, we celebrate the graduation of our daughter, Cora Lee, from high school. *(He toasts MARGRIT'S glass, holds his high in the air and booms the word in triumph)* VALEVICDORIAN!

MARGRIT
Vale-DIC-TOR-ian, honey.

FRANKLIN

Well, whatever you call it. I just know she the number one student coming out of that high school, I know that. And, I know that with the help of God, another one done graduated. She'll be the second child we send off to college, and only the Lord know how proud we is. *(To CORA LEE)* Come here, girl. *(FRANKLIN and MARGRIT embrace CORA LEE. The guests applaud. Looking at CORA LEE..)* You can be a handful sometimes, but I still wish your grandma could be here to see you today. She'd be so proud of you. So proud. *(He is quiet for a moment, reflecting.)* My mama couldn't read or write, you know, on account of she didn't never have no chance to go to school. All she knowed was them tobacco fields. And, me, too, really cause I wasn't seeing too much of the insides of a schoolhouse my own self. Wasn't nobody's fault, that's just the way thangs was back then. But, one day when me and her was coming home from them fields, walking down that long winding country road in near-dark, I looked at my mama, old before her time, always as tired as an old mule, and I promised myself two thangs that day.

I say to myself that day, I don't care how many chil'ren I have, I'm gonna name every last one of them after my mama. Her name was Lee. Lee Turner. She was named after a slave who saved her Daddy's life. Took a whipping for him. Anyway, today we got Jonathan Lee, Cora Lee, and David Lee. I can't say my chil'ren's name without thinking 'bout my mama. And, that's the way it's supposed to be. So, I done the first thang. The second thang I promised myself was that if I had to work *ten* jobs, my chil'ren would not just know how to read and write, like me, but they'd be educated somebodies. Y'all know what I mean?

DAVID LEE

How long is this speech going to last, Daddy? The food's getting cold. *(The guest laugh. MARGRIT hushes DAVID LEE.)*

FRANKLIN

Well, the second reason we celebrating is because our son, Jonathan Lee, just come home from school. He finished his second year of law school. *(As the guest applaud, he calls JONATHAN.)* Welcome home, boy! And, if God's willing, David Lee'll be going to high school in a few years. Come on over here, boy. *(He embraces all three children.)* I'd give my right arm for Mama to be here and see these chil'ren. I didn't 'mount to much, but, Lord, look at these chil'ren. Look at these chil'ren! If Mama was here, she wouldn't know *what* to say. *(He stops speaking, overcome with emotion.)* Hell, I don't know what to say my own self.

DAVID LEE

You sure said a lot, Daddy. Not to know what to say.

FRANKLIN

Well, the only thang I'm gonna say now is: Y'all eat, drink and let the good times roll! Put on that music, Tyree. *(He grabs MARGRIT and they begin to dance as sounds of rhythm and blues music comes up on the record player. As soon as the music come up, it begins to fade to become soft background music. The party goes on inside, as JONATHAN and CORA LEE go outside onto the porch. The rest of the stage darkens although the music can be heard* inside, *playing softly. The music has now been changed to a softer sound, which plays throughout JONATHAN and CORA LEE's conversation.)*

JONATHAN

(On porch with CORA LEE) Man, it was worth every night I stayed up late studying just to see him so proud.

CORA LEE

I'm surprised he's still proud of me. After what's happened.

JONATHAN
Yeah, he sure was upset when he had to drive all the way out to Mills County to bail you out of jail that last time. I thought he was going to have a stroke or something. You know how strange he looked. Remember?

CORA LEE
(Guiltily) Yeah, I remember.

JONATHAN
We haven't had much time to really talk since I've been home, Corrie – what with the graduation and – and…

CORA LEE
And me being in jail all the time. Don't be afraid to say it.

JONATHAN
Yeah, with you being in jail all the time. But I did promise mama I'd talk to you.

CORA LEE
Save your breath, Jon. I'm not interested.

JONATHAN
If you're not interested in sparing them the pain, Corrie, at least think about yourself. This stuff you're doing is going to interfere with any plans for college.

CORA LEE
Living under these Jim Crow laws is interfering with all my plans for life, Jonathan. Have you thought about that?

JONATHAN
Hey! I'm serious, Corrie. What if you go out there and get badly hurt? Or, what if you can't get bail. Either one might jeopardize your chances of going to college.

CORA LEE

Then I won't go to college. And, I'm serious, too.

JONATHAN

(Shocked) What! Not go to college! Cora Lee Turner, what's come over you? You know Mama and Dad have planned their whole life for us to go to college. You saw him just now. So proud of us. It would destroy him if you didn't go.

CORA LEE

(Pensively) Jonathan, sometimes I think I'm not going to make it to college.

JONATHAN

What! What are you talking about, Corrie. It's less than two months away. Of course you'll make it. It's all set, isn't it? The scholarship and everything?

CORA LEE

Everything's all arranged, but --- but--- for some reason it seems so far away. So far that I'll never get there.

JONATHAN

(Putting arms around her) Of course you'll get there, silly. And, you'll love campus life, with your adventuresome spirit and that burning desire you have for learning. It's where you belong, Corrie. *(He lifts her chin and looks into her eyes.)* O.K., Corrie-Porrie?

CORA LEE

(Laughing at his childhood nickname for her) O.K. Jonnie-Ponnie.

JONATHAN
(Staring at her for a while) Was it bad in jail?

CORA LEE
(After thinking about it for a while) Yes and no. Yes, it was smelly and uncomfortable and the food was absolutely horrible, but I think we all transcended that. You know what I mean? Everybody's spirit was so high, nothing could bring us down. We told jokes, sang songs and laughed a lot.

JONATHAN
Jokes!

CORA LEE
Yeah, we told jokes.

JONATHAN
How could you laugh in that filth, behind bars?

CORA LEE
The jokes were funny! *(They laugh.)* What was happening to our bodies was unimportant. Our minds were above it all. *(She is quiet a moment.)* Something happened to me in there, Jon. Something strange.

JONATHAN
(Alarmed) What? Did somebody bother you?

CORA LEE
No, nothing like that. Something different. I don't even know if I can explain it. *(She falls silent.)*

JONATHAN
Try.

CORA LEE

That night in Mills County Jail, after I fell asleep, I had a weird dream. I dreamt the word "We." That's all W-E. All night, my sleeping mind said, "We." And when I woke up, the first thing that came to my mind was "We."

JONATHAN

"We? The word, we?"

CORA LEE

Yes, we. *(Pauses)* When I woke up I wondered what it meant. And the second I wondered, it came to me, like a revelation or something. You see, before I had fallen asleep, we had been singing "We Shall Overcome". You know that's an old Negro spiritual, Jon, and I had always thought that the "we" of that song was us – our people. But, when I woke up that morning in jail, it came to me that "we" is all of us, Jon. It's all the people in this country, not just Negroes and not just whites, either. It's all the people in the world. We. WE shall overcome. Injustice is an evil, but it's not just an evil for those who are the victims of it. It's also an evil for those who force it upon others. And when that idea came to me, I realized that I've been hearing the same thing all during school in different ways but hadn't connected it. Remember, "No man is an island?" And, John Donne said, "Any man's death diminishes me, for I am concerned with mankind." Don't you understand? Mankind is all connected, somehow, Jon. We. We is all of us, the whole world. People everywhere. We. And, *we* must all overcome this hatred, this disease or we are all doomed.

Then when I thought of that, another thought became clear. Crystal clear. If "we" really does mean all the people of the world, then that means that we – we in that jail – our side was going to win, because that means that there has to be millions, millions of people on our side – on the side of right – on the side of good – on the side of justice. Millions, Jon. We! Don't you understand?

JONATHAN

Well....

CORA LEE

I was thinking about it so hard, I started to see it. I could actually see it, Jon! And when I saw it, I was so happy, I started to cry. It was real crowded in the cell we were in and Tyree was right next to me and Tee. When I started to cry, Tyree said, "Don't be scared, Corrie." And I said, "I'm not scared, Tyree. I'm happy." Then, he said, "Happy?" And, I said, "Yes, I'm happy because I'm having a vision." Tyree said, "Don't be cracking up in here, girl. It's too crowded, and you know we can't get out of here." Everybody sort of stepped back, to give me a little room, but I didn't care. I could see it.

JONATHAN

(Quietly) What did you see?

CORA LEE

We, Jon. That's what I saw. We. We will come from all over the state… all over this country, from all around the world. Negroes and whites, Jews and Gentiles, young and old, Northerners and Southerners. We are coming and we will fill the jails of this land, Jon. We'll be marching hand in hand. We'll be marching for justice. That's what I saw.

JONATHAN

Do you really think that some white people are going to march or go to jail for you, Corrie?

CORA LEE

I saw it!

JONATHAN

It's just that over active imagination of yours.

CORA LEE
No, Jon, it's going to happen.

JONATHAN
If something like that ever did happen, it would change this entire country. But, I don't think anything like that will ever happen. I wish I did, Corrie, but I just don't.

CORA LEE
That's because you don't understand about We, Jon. Everybody's been busy dividing folks up as black or white or red or yellow when all along we should have been divided up as good or evil, just or unjust, right or wrong. Because there's good and bad in all groups. But, the vast majority of people are good, Jon. I know that now.

JONATHAN
If I really thought that your vision would come true, maybe I would try non-violent resistance myself. But, since I don't believe it will work, I find it foolhardy to compromise my ethics by being arrested and jailed. *(Pauses)* Don't you?

CORA LEE
Everyone fights injustice in the manner that he sees fit, Jon. I won't criticize your methods if don't criticize mine.

CURTAIN

ACT II
SCENE 2

Time: Two weeks later.
Place: Turner's living room.

(MARGRIT is sitting on sofa and FRANKLIN is lying, his head resting on MARGRIT's lap. They are watching television. The news announcer is broadcasting news about the civil rights protests. The announcer is heard, not seen.)

VOICE OF TELEVISION ANNOUNCER
(Off Stage)... Today, there are reports of several sit-ins in drugstores across the South. In Selma, seventeen students have been arrested today for sitting at a lunch counter in Walview Drugstore. Authorities are concerned because of the line of Negroes waiting to go inside to replace those arrested. The sheriff states that space is not a problem at this time, however...

FRANKLIN
(To Margrit) You hear that? *(The doorbell rings)* Come in.

THERESA
(Enters) Hello, Mr. and Mrs. Turner.

FRANKLIN
Hi, Theresa

MARGRIT
(Slipping from under FRANKLIN and standing up) Hello, Theresa. How are you, dear? Can I offer you something cool to drink? I just made a big pitcher of ice cold lemonade.

THERESA
Thank you, Mrs. Turner. I don't mind if I do.

MARGRIT

(To FRANKLIN) Would you like a glass, honey?

FRANKLIN

Thanks, baby. Sounds good to me. **(MARGRIT EXITS. FRANKLIN gets up, turns down the volume on the television. He returns and sits on sofa, interested in the news)** If somebody had told me the day would come when Negroes would line up to go to jail, I would of thought they was drunk, crazy or both. Lord! This beats all. *(Pointing to T.V. set)* Did you hear that?

THERESA

Yes, sir, I heard it.

FRANKLIN

Don't make *no* kind of sense to me. They get arrested, pay all that money for bail, have to keep running back to court and for what? Nothing's going to change. Them folks been sitting up at them lunch counters for over a month and the stores still saying, "Niggers, don't sit down here," *(To THERESA)* What's the point of all this? *(He gestures towards the television)*

CORA LEE

(Has entered while FRANKLIN was talking. She answers question he has just asked THERESA) The drugstores are losing a lot of money.

FRANKLIN

Yeah, they're losing money, but, that's not changing nothing. It's not changing the laws.

CORA LEE

(Softly, emphatically) But, it will, Daddy. Watch and see. One day, all over this country, colored people will sit wherever they want on

a bus, and eat wherever they want and maybe even live wherever they want.

FRANKLIN
(Drily) And, maybe even get lynched wherever they want. Since they choosing so much.

MARGRIT
(Entering with a tray containing glasses of lemonade) Here's the lemonade, it's cold and sweet. And let's stop all this race talk. It's so unpleasant. *(To CORA LEE)* Would you like a glass, Cora Lee? I can get another glass for myself. *(She holds glass out to CORA LEE)*

CORA LEE
No, thanks, Mama. We've got to be going.

DAVID LEE
(ENTERS. Taking glass from MARGRIT's hand in passing by) Thanks, Mama!

MARGRIT
David Lee! You're bleeding! *(She inspects his wound)*

FRANKLIN
(Quickly) What did they do to him?

DAVID LEE
They who? It was just Willie Tee.

MARGRIT
(Visually relieved) What happened?

DAVID LEE
I had a fight with Willie Tee, that's all.

MARGRIT
What on earth would you and Willie Tee fight about?

DAVID LEE
(Defensively) He started it, Mama. He said the white folks was going to kill Cora Lee – her out there trying to integrate with them and stuff. I told him they weren't going to kill her nothing. Then, he said his daddy said white folks gonna have Cora Lee swinging from a tree with her tongue hanging out the side of her mouth. And, then, he said some more stuff, Mama. Say his daddy said it. So, I told him his daddy was idle-brained. Then, he got mad and started talking about you, Mama.

MARGRIT
Me?

DAVID LEE
Yeah, he said last Sunday you wore some purple polka dotted high heel gym shoes, some raggedy bloomers and a blond wig to church. So, I punched him in the nose. Nobody's gonna talk about my Mama and my sister to my face.

THERESA
Willie Tee's just silly. That sounds like something Willie Tee would say.

FRANKLIN
Signifying! That's what he's doing.

DAVID LEE

I know it. Signifying about you like that, Mama. Lying about Corrie too.

FRANKLIN

I done told you about listening to that fool.

MARGRIT

You know we don't want you fighting, young man. Especially over some nonsense like that.

DAVID LEE

But, that's not fair, Mama! I was just telling the truth about his daddy and he got mad and started signifying about my mama. That's not fair!

MARGRIT

(Sharply) Do you think your father's idle-brained? *(Pauses)* Well, do you?

DAVID LEE

No, ma'am.

MARGRIT

And, Willie Tee doesn't think that his father's idled-brained either, David lee. He believes what his father says, just like you believe what your father says. That's only natural. *(Turning to give FRANKLIN a glaring look)* That's why it's so important what grown folks say, or don't say, in front of children.

FRANKLIN

Don't be rolling your eyes back here at me, woman, cause I know better than to say just anythang in front of chil'ren. But, I don't see no reason to be tip-toeing around whispering that a fool's a fool.

Especially when everybody know it anyway. And that fool know it his own self.

MARGRIT
But his boy doesn't know it, Franklin. Every child has a right to believe in his parents.

FRANKLIN
Even if they a fool, huh?

MARGRIT
Especially if they're a fool.

FRANKLIN
Well, I know one thang. That fool's little fool keep messing with my boy, he going to be a black-eyed fool. Cause David Lee going to put a hurt on him. Ain't you, David Lee?

DAVID LEE
I turned him every which way but loose, Daddy.

FRANKLIN
Gone, boy!

MARGRIT
I still don't want you out there fighting like some common hoodlum.

FRANKLIN
Yeah, he keep on signifying about this family, David Lee going to common hoodlum him.

DAVID LEE
I know his nose is looking mighty funny.

FRANKLIN

Gone, boy!

MARGRIT

Franklin, don't encourage your own child to fight. Teach him how to compromise differences. Use his brain, not his fists.

FRANKLIN

A boy ain't like a girl, Margrit. A boy's got to learn to take care of his own self. Especially a colored one.

CORA LEE

(Going to DAVID LEE. Tenderly) I don't want you fighting either, David Lee, but it sure warms my heart to know you'd fight for my honor and that you care whether I get killed or not.

DAVID LEE

Sure I care! If you get killed, I'll have to do all the dishes by myself.

CORA LEE

Sure, Mr. Cover Up. But it's too late. *(She kisses him on the cheek)* I got the message already. Bye, now.

MARGRIT

You're not going downtown, are you? With all that mess and confusion going on down there.

CORA LEE

Yes, we are.

MARGRIT

Where downtown?

CORA LEE

We're going to Walview Drugstore.

FRANKLIN

(Stops watching television and glances at CORA LEE) What for?

CORA LEE

I'm going to buy a Pepsi and Tee's buying a Coke-Cola.

MAGRIT

(Understanding) Why would you girls go all the way downtown to buy soft drinks when we have all the lemonade you want right here?

CORA LEE

We're not thirsty, Mama. We're hungry.

DAVID LEE

I'm hungry and thirsty.

MARGRIT

Well, that's a problem I can solve easily. I have a big pot of greens, piping hot on the stove and fried chicken and corn...

CORA LEE

We're hungry for justice, Mama. We're going to another sit-in.

FRANKLIN

(Jumps to his feet, shouting) Like hell you are!

DAVID LEE

Here we go again.

CORA LEE

Daddy, I was hoping you'd understand by now.

FRANKLIN

Then, you was hoping wrong!

CORA LEE

(Sadly) Daddy, I've got to go.

MARGRIT

Stop her, Franklin. Don't let her go.

FRANKLIN

(Goes to CORA LEE, grabs her arm and holds it. His voice is angry) I said you're not going, dammit, and I mean just that!

CORA LEE

(Crying, but still determined) I have to go out there every day and fight those rednecks. Now, I've got to fight you, too. *(Frustrated)* Why!?!

FRANKLIN

(Forcefully) Cause we don't want you dead!

CORA LEE

(Coldly, wanting to hurt, as she jerks arm away) Maybe if you had used a little of your strength on them, I wouldn't have to fight them now! *(FRANKLIN raises hand to slap her, then stops in mid-air turns and walks slowly to window, stares out. Silence hangs heavily in the room)*

MARGRIT

(To CORA LEE) How dare you! How dare you! As sure as hell exists or God Almighty sits in His throne in Heaven, your father

can't fight night-riders, Klu Klux Klan, or the sheriff, because they've got the law on their side. But one-on-one, he can whip any man in this town, black or white and probably kill them with his bare hands! Don't you dare try to even suggest that he's not strong! You feeling yourself, too womanish for me and I'm fed up with it. I'm tired of trying to reason with you. You've been to jail for the last time, Cora Lee! You're not going back! We're not working our fingers to the bones to raise a jailbird. (*Pauses*) That man's been working two jobs for the past seven years so that you can live in this nice house and have food, and you children can go to school. And you think you have a right to stand up in his house and defy him to his face? And make innuendoes about his manhood! Huh! Going crazy is one thing, girl, but this kind of disrespect is something we're not going to have in this house! Not today! Not tomorrow! Not ever!

CORA LEE
(*Contritely. Turning to face FRANKLIN who is still looking out of the window. Talking to his back. She is so contrite for having insulted him that she is on the verge of tears.*) Daddy, … Daddy, I… Daddy, I didn't…

FRANKLIN
(*Interrupting her, but not turning around. Speaking to DAVID LEE*) David Lee, go into my bedroom and bring me that little knotty pine box on the dresser.

DAVID LEE
The one you keep your important papers in?

FRANKLIN
(*Still not turning around*) That's the one, son.

(As DAVID LEE exits, FRANKLIN goes and sits on sofa. CORA LEE heads towards him, but DAVID LEE comes back and gets to FRANKLIN first. He gives FRANKLIN the box.)

DAVID LEE

Here it is, Daddy.

FRANKLIN

(FRANKLIN opens box, looks through it. He finds what he's looking for, takes it out, closes box and sits it on the end table and sits holding the object he has taken out of the box.) I never told you the story behind this, did I, Cora Lee?

CORA LEE

(Coming closer, looking down to see what he's holding. Puzzled) It's a one-hundred dollar bill!

FRANKLIN

Yeah, but not just any hundred dollar bill. This one is special. *(He stares into space remembering the past)* You remember Mac, don't you, honey? Use to live over on Old Lexington Road?

CORA LEE

(Wanting to show respect) Yes sir. A little.

FRANKLIN

(Going back into his reverie) Mac and me – we growed up together on neighboring farms. Both our folks sharecropping. When we was boys, we'd get together every chance we could -- which wasn't much, considering we had to work them fields all the time. But, sometimes, we'd find time to swing on some swings we made out of old tires and rope.

Once in a while we'd get a chance to go fishing. I oughta say Mac went fishing. All I did was drown some worms, cause I

93

never caught a datblame fish. I remember we had a couple of old rusty tire rims we usta roll around with a stick. Anythang to try to have some fun. No such thang as toys back then. You know where old man Perkins' store is, David Lee?

DAVID LEE
Yes, sir.

FRANKLIN
Well, before that store was there, that land was just a big old field. Everybody called it Old man Perkins Place. Old Man Perkins had a old water hole back of this place. Me and Mac usta sneak over there and go swimming. *(Laughs)* You ever see anybody trying to put on some clothes – running? That's what we did when old man Perkins came running with his shot gun. Boy! Don't let nobody tell you, you can't do two thangs at the same time. Me and Mac could run and get dressed like nobody's business. *(He laughs, remembering)* We sho' had some fun back then, me and Mac. We growed on...

CORA LEE
(Interrupting him) Daddy. I've got to go...

FRANKLIN
(Ignoring her, his voice drowning her out) ... up and I went to work for the railroad. I was a big old husky thang and I wanted to work outdoors, but not in no cotton or tobacco fields. Mac joined the army and went off to war. He always did like adventure. Anyway, over in Europe, he got both his legs busted up, saving two white soldiers' lives. They give Mac a Purple Heart and Mac come on back home. I remember like it was yesterday, the day I met him at the train station.

CORA LEE
(Impatiently) I know about Mr. Mac's legs, Daddy. Everybody knows he had bad legs and walked with a limp.

FRANKLIN
(Seemingly oblivious to her impatience) If he had been white, I guess he would have been the town's hero. But, the best this town could do for him was offer Mac a job as a janitor at city hall.

CORA LEE
Daddy, it's getting late.

FRANKLIN
Mac took the job, he had a wife and four chil'ren to take care of -- - then something bad happened.

MARGRIT
David Lee, go in the kitchen and shell those peas on the table.

DAVID LEE
Aw, I want to hear what bad thing happened!

MARGRIT
Go on, you heard me.

DAVID LEE
Aw, shoot. I always miss the good part.

MARGRIT
I'm not going to tell you again.

DAVID LEE
Aw, Mama, *(Leaving)*

FRANKLIN

Let him stay, Margrit. He's old enough to know what he's up against down here. He can shell them peas in here. *(David Lee rushes out rear to get peas)* They've been killing black boys down here for a long time. *(David Lee is just coming back. Stops dismayed at MARGRIT's words.)*

MARGRIT

Wash your hands first.

DAVID LEE

(Stops, goes back) Aw, Mama.

FRANKLIN

This thing happened about eight years back. Mac was on his way home from his job at city hall one day. Some days his legs would hurt like hell and he told me later that this was one of them days. Mac got on the bus, paid his fare and went on to the back of the bus. The back section was filled up so Mac had to stand up. There was empty seats in the front, but Mac knowed the front of the bus was for whites only. *(Pauses. David Lee has returned in a flurry at the start of this tale and is listening intently from the dining room table where he is shelling peas.)* So Mac stood up on the back of the bus on his hurting legs. At the next stop, enough white people got on to fill up the white section and a colored woman got off and Mac sat down in the seat. It was the first seat in the colored section.

THERESA

(Understanding the implication) Oh, no!

FRANKLIN

At the next stop, two young white boys, about sixteen, big, blond, husky farm boys got on. They looked around in the white section for a seat, then come on back to the back --- to Mac. One of the boys ordered Mac and the woman sitting next to him to get up and give them they seats. The woman got on up but Mac just sat there.

MARGRIT
Oh, God!

FRANKLIN
Now, that white boy knowed he was supposed to tell the bus driver, and the bus driver would have had Mac arrested right off. And, Mac knowed he was supposed to, by law, get up and give his seat to that white boy – but neither one did what they knowed they was supposed to do that day.

CORA LEE
Daddy, please. I've got to…

FRANKLIN
(Still ignoring her) The white boy grabbed Mac and start trying to throw him on the floor! Mac hauled off and slammed his fist into that redneck's face so hard, it knocked the boy down. Mac say that boy looked up at him like he was a crazy man done escaped from the crazy house.

CORA LEE
Good for Mac!

DAVID LEE
(Cheering) Yeah!!

FRANKLIN
(Sadly) Yeah, good for Mac. Mac was arrested and threw into jail. He was fired from his job at city hall, his wife, Leah was fired from her job doing housework and their house was burnt down. All this happened in three days.

CORA LEE

Oh, my God!

FRANKLIN

When Mac finally got out of jail and went home, Leah and the chil'ren just standing in the yard. House gone. Everythang gone. They'd been sleeping on the ground since the day he'd refused to give up his seat.

CORA LEE

Didn't they have insurance on the house?

FRANKLIN

Yeah, I guess they did. The insurance company told them they didn't pay up for no houses deliberately set on fire.

CORA LEE

What time is it, Tee?

THERESA

Three twenty-one.

FRANKLIN

Mac told the insurance people that he didn't set the fire and didn't know who had, but they wouldn't pay him a solitary dime.

CORA LEE

Daddy, we're going to miss our group if we don't go, now.

FRANKLIN

(Still ignoring her) I went over to his place – where it had been anyway--. They was just standing in the yard. I say, "Why you do it, Mac? Why didn't you just… just… stand up, man?" *(Looks up into Cora Lee's face)* You know what he say?

98

CORA LEE

I've got to go now, Daddy.

FRANKLIN

He say, "Franklin, man. I was just tired." *(He stands)* I say, "Hell, man. Ain't the first time a nigger's been tired. Why didn't you just stand up?" *(Walks over to Cora Lee, looks her in the face)* He say, "I was tired of being tired." *(He looks at the bill in his hands)* I had saved up a hundred dollars, bit by bit. I come on home and got it. I went back and give it to Mac. I ask him, what he was going to do now. He say, "I'm gonna leave this place." And, he did. *(He goes back to sofa, sits)* One day, about three years later, I get a letter from Baltimore. Now, I don't know a soul in Baltimore. But this mail came – inside just this hundred dollar bill wrapped in a clean piece of paper... No writing inside nowhere. No name, no address, no nothing. But I knowed who sent it. I knowed. I saved it all these years. I always felt I should keep it for something special. Nothing special ever come along.

CORA LEE

Daddy, I'm going, now. *(Turns to leave)*

MARGRIT

No, Cora Lee!

FRANKLIN

(Shouting) Cora Lee! *(She stops, but does not turn around. He speaks to her back)* Do you think this Dr. Hicks person is the first somebody to break one of them Jim Crow laws?

CORA LEE

No, sir.

FRANKLIN

Hundreds of us have broke them laws. Just like Mac did. But, everyone I know of was crushed.

CORA LEE

(Calmly) That's because the other Negroes didn't help them after they broke them.

FRANKLIN

(Angrily) When you was arrested, didn't your Mama and me come bail you out? Didn't we take you to the hearing? Driving thirty miles to Mills County that last time. What more can we do?

CORA LEE

(Turning to face him, exasperated) You can come help us fill the jails, Daddy! That's the only way they'll change those laws.

FRANKLIN

(Shouting) They won't change them, Cora Lee!

CORA LEE

(Shouting back) Then, you change! You change, Daddy! You change, Mama! Be what you are, not what they want you to be! *(She heads for the door)*

FRANKLIN

(He grabs her and slings her away from the door) You leave here over my dead body! *(She tries to run past him, he stops her, a struggle ensues)* You might as well go on without her, Theresa, cause she ain't going.

CORA LEE

(Struggling) I've got to go. I've got to go.

THRESA

Please let her go, Mr. Turner.

FRANKLIN

(He slings Cora Lee onto sofa) You ain't going. Leave, Theresa. She ain't going!

THERESA

(Turning to leave) I'm sorry, Corrie. I'll tell them you tried to come.

CORA LEE

(She tries one last time to leave. She manages to get off the sofa, but FRANKLIN catches her and holds her. She struggles to no avail. She calls around him to THERESA, who is leaving) Tell them I'll come tomorrow.

FRANKLIN

Don't tell them no such lie!

CORA LEE

(Crying, pounding on his chest with her fists) I want to go to jail. I want to go to jail.

FRANKLIN

(Suddenly he lets CORA LEE go, clutches his chest stumbles across the room) Oh, God! Oh, God! *(He falls to floor. All present including CORA LEE call out his name and run to him)*

CURTAIN

ACT III
SCENE 1

Time: Saturday afternoon, almost a week later.
Place: The Turners' living room.

(The house light dim and we hear the unmistakable playing of David Lee. The CURTAINS open to MARGRIT and MRS. BLACKWELL in living room listening to DAVID LEE play. He finish and they applaud.)

MRS. BLACKWELL
Thank you so much, David Lee. Your playing is so beautiful I could just sit here and listen to it all day long.

DAVID LEE
(Fearful) But, I can't play all day, Mrs. Blackwell. I've got to...

MRS. BLACKWELL
Boy, you know I ain't fool enough to expect you to sit here playing that piano for some old lady, all day. I was just complimenting you, that's all. You run on about your business.

DAVID LEE
Mama, may I watch television?

MARGRIT
Not now, David Lee. I have company.

DAVID LEE
But Gunsmoke is coming on.

MARGRIT
What time does it come on?

DAVID LEE

Four o'clock.

MARGRIT

(Looking at watch) That's an hour from now.

DAVID LEE

But, I want to be ready. I don't want to miss it.

MARGRIT

No, you find something else to do until four o'clock. I've got company now. Go feed the dog.

DAVID LEE

(Dejectedly) I already fed him.

MARGRIT

Go clean your room.

DAVID LEE

I'll feed him again. *(Exits)*

MARGRIT

That boy. He'll be the death of me yet.

MRS. BLACKWELL

How's Franklin doing, Margrit?

MARGRIT

He's just fine, Mrs. Blackwell. Yesterday the doctors said he'll have to give up his second job. Two hard jobs at his age would give anybody a heart attack, they say.

MRS. BLACKWELL
Just praise the Lord the heart attack didn't kill him.

MARGRIT
I do praise the Lord. I praise Him every day. I'll just be glad when Franklin gets home from the hospital.

CORA LEE
(Enters. Followed by DAVID LEE. She has changed. There is an overwhelming melancholy that has overcome her, as though her life spirit has been drained away. Her speech and actions throughout this scene are lifeless and mechanical.) Hello, Mrs. Blackwell.

MRS. BLACKWELL
(Gaily, in contrast to CORA LEE) Why, hello, Coral Lee! How are you doing today, child?

CORA LEE
Fine.

MARGRIT
Cora Lee! Where's your manners, girl. You didn't even ask Mrs. Blackwell how she's doing.

CORA LEE
How're you doing, Mrs. Blackwell?

MRS. BLACKWELL
(Looking closely at CORA LEE, seeing the change) I'm doing just fine, Cora Lee. I'm still kicking.

CORA LEE
Mama, I'm going now. *(Goes to front door)*

DAVID LEE

Where are you going in that dress with those big old polka-dots?

CORA LEE

Choir practice.

DAVID LEE

Choir practice? I thought you had quit that stuff?

CORA LEE

I joined again.

DAVID LEE

Aren't you going to get mad at me like you always do when I poke fun at your polka-dot dress?

CORA LEE

(Quietly) No.

DAVID LEE

What's the matter, Corrie?

CORA LEE

Nothing.

DAVID LEE

(Enthusiastically) Want a bite of my candy bar?

CORA LEE

No.

DAVID LEE

I got another one in my room that I didn't even bite out of. You want it?

CORA LEE

No.

DAVID LEE

You're not going to beg me to play your favorite song for you? It's Saturday.

CORA LEE

I'm going now.

DAVID LEE

(Putting hand on her arm to stop her) Am I still Orpheus?

CORA LEE

(This seems to bring her out of the deep trance-like state, although melancholy still governs her. She touches his face, kisses him on the forehead, then, looks into his eyes) You'll always be Orpheus. *(To Margrit)* Mama, I'm going now.

MARGRIT

(Coming to *doorway*) I'll see you when you get back.

CORA LEE

When Tee comes, tell her I'm…I'm.. not going. I called to tell her myself, but no one answered the phone.

MARGRIT

I'll tell her. *(Pauses)* Cora Lee, wait. *(Another pause)* This is for the best, dear. Yesterday they were using electric cattle prods on those protesters.

CORA LEE

Bye, mama *(Exits)*

DAVID LEE
May I watch television now, Mama? I'm going to miss the show.

MARGRIT
(Looking at watch) It's not time yet.

DAVID LEE
Shoot! *(Goes to piano, strike three angry chords, stalks out, bumping Into JONATHAN who is entering living room)*

JONATHAN
Hey, what's wrong with him?

MARGRIT
Just being mannish, that's all.

JONATHAN
Hello Mrs. Blackwell. How are you, today?

MRS. BLACKWELL
Hello, Jonathan Lee. I'm just fine, boy. I'm still kicking.

JONATHAN
Where's Corrie, Mama? I'm going to see if she wants to go to the hospital with me to see Dad.

MARGRIT
She's gone to choir practice, Jonathan. She joined the choir again. Praise the Lord!

JONATHAN
She joined the choir again?

MARGRIT

She sure did. I always knew she was a good girl.

JONATHAN

(**Angrily**) She's always been a good girl. You knew that all along.

MARGRIT

What are you so mad about?

JONATHAN

(*Shouting*) I'm not mad!

MARGRIT

Something must be in the air. All you children acting like... (*The doorbell rings, interrupting her*) Come in!

THERESA

Hello, Mrs. Turner, Mrs. Blackwell. How are you today? Hi, Jon.

MARGRIT

Hello, Theresa.

MRS. BLACKWELL

Hey there, Theresa Browser. I'm fine, girl. Still kicking.

MARGRIT

Cora Lee phoned you, Theresa. No one answered. She told me to tell you she's not going.

THERESA

(*Shocked*) Not going?

JONATHAN

I'm leaving, now, Mama. Good-bye, Mrs. Blackwell. See ya,
Theresa.

MRS. BLACKWELL

Good-bye, boy.

THERESA

Bye, Jon.

MARGRIT

(To Jonathan) Tell your father we send our love. We'll all be over
there right after church tomorrow to see him. Be sure to tell him
now.

JONATHAN

I'll tell him. *(Exists)*

DAVID LEE

*(Has re-entered. Comes over to doorway where MARGRIT and
THERESA are standing)* Is it time, yet?

MARGRIT

I still have company.

DAVID LEE

(In too-loud whisper) When is she going home?

MARGRIT

Shh.

DAVID LEE

Oh, hi, Theresa.

THERESA

Hi, David Lee.

MRS. BLACKWELL

(Coming to doorway) It's time for me to be going, Margrit. It's getting close to my nap time. I'll see you young'uns, later. Yeah, I might have to take a nap every day, but I'm still kicking. *(Exits)*

DAVID LEE

(MARGRIT, THERESA and DAVID LEE all wave good-bye with DAVID LEE showing the most enthusiasm) Good-bye, Mrs. Blackwell. *Bye!* *(Lowers voice, still waving)* Bye. I didn't think she was ever going to go home.

MARGRIT

David Lee!

DAVID LEE

Can I watch television, now?

MARGRIT

May I watch television, now?

DAVID LEE

(Correcting himself simultaneously) May I watch television now?

MARGRIT

Just keep the volume down. I'm going to be on the porch talking to Theresa. *(MARGRIT and THERESA go onto porch)*

DAVID LEE

(Runs to turn on television, sprawls on floor in front of set) It's about time!

THERESA

(On porch with MARGRIT) I don't understand about Corrie. Why she's not going.

MARGRIT

You know they used electric cattle prods on those protesters yesterday, don't you?

THERESA

That wouldn't stop Corrie from going.

MARGRIT

It would stop anybody with some sense from going.

THERESA

(Calmly) Corrie has gone through fear, Mrs. Turner. She's on the other side.

MARGRIT

There is no other side of fear. You're either facing it or in it. And ironically, fear is one of our most protective emotions. It's what keeps us safe.

THERESA

It's also what enslaves us, sometimes.

MARGRIT

Somebody needs to try to talk some sense into you, Theresa. With those white people using dogs, water hoses, and cattle prods, the only thing that can happen is somebody is going to get hurt. Real bad. And, it won't be them.

THERESA

Did she say she'd go tomorrow?

MARGRIT

She didn't say that, but she's not. Cora Lee's through with all that mess, Theresa. She's at choir practice now, and tomorrow morning we're going to church, then we're going to the hospital to visit her father. She really doesn't have time for that nonsense.

THERESA

(Disappointed) Oh.

MARGRIT

The doctors said that another heart attack like the one Franklin had will kill him. Cora Lee knows...
(A sudden loud, searing wail is heard from inside. It is a cry that is born of horror and fear. The second time it comes, it can almost be distinguished as being the word "mama.")

DAVID LEE

Mama! Mama!
(MARGRIT and THERESA run inside to the living room. DAVID LEE is on his knees in front of the television. He is obviously in a state of shock. He continues to moan, in a keening manner, the only word he seems capable of saying, "mama" over and over)

DAVID LEE

Mama, mama, mama, mamamamamamamamamamama.....

MARGRIT

David Lee! David Lee! What's the matter! What's wrong with you? *(She is all around him, trying to see if he is hurt. She is bewildered. Her eyes, in their frantic search, happen to cross the path of the television screen. She does a double take and stare into the screen. She reaches over, in slow motion, and turns up*

112

the volume on the television. We hear the voice of the news announcer.)

VOICE OF TELEVISION NEWS ANNOUNCER

…and there is complete chaos here. I repeat, there has been a bombing at the Morial Street Baptist Church at the corner of Main and Morial Streets. It is reported that about thirty children were in the church at the time of the bombing. Twenty-five have been accounted for, most having some kind of injury. Although the church is still burning, firemen are fighting their way inside, hoping to rescue the others. So far, three bodies have been recovered.

THERESA

(Hysterically) Oh, my God! Oh, my God! They bombed the church! They bombed the church!

MARGRIT

(She is trapped in the midst of fear. It is a place she has never been before. Her brain is frozen on two words, which she chants almost incoherently) God, please! God, please! God, please! Please! Please! Please, God, please, please, please. Please, God. Please. God, please, please. God, please!

THERESA

(Theresa has been screaming pathetically. Her thoughts return to her enough for her to think what to do) I'm going to the church! *(Exists running)*

MARGRIT

(The slamming of the screen door diverts her momentarily. She looks at the door, reacting to its sudden sound. She runs from the room, saying one last word) Please!

DAVID LEE

(He is still chanting, "Mama." Staring at the television screen. He begins to back away on his knees from the horror he is seeing, unable to stop looking. Suddenly he jumps to his feet. Holding his head back, he shrieks to the top of his voice) MAMA! *(He exits, running. We are left with the voice of the television announcer repeating his tale of woe.)*

CURTAIN

ACT III
SCENE 2

(Once the curtains close, all lights dim to black. Total darkness ensues. This is the funeral. Attendance for the audience is mandatory. Out of the darkness we hear the voice of a choir singing a single word.

VOICE OF CHOIR
(Singing) A-men!

VOICE OF CHOIR
(Singing) Allelujah! Allelujah! Allelujah! A- le- a – lu- a- jah! (*As the minister speaks, the choir repeats the words. "Forever and ever – Hallelujah, Hallelujah" between his verses)*

VOICE OF MINISTER
Oh give thanks unto the Lord: for He is good: for His mercy endureth forever.
Oh give thanks unto the God of god: for His mercy endureth forever.
Oh give thanks to the Lord of lords: for His mercy endureth forever.
Who remembered us in our low estate: for His mercy endureth forever.
Oh give thanks unto the God of heaven: for His mercy endureth forever. *(Pauses)*
Now, the eulogy will be delivered by Theresa Browser.

VOICE OF THERESA
After one of our meetings one day, where the topic was Fear and Death, Corrie gave me this poem and said, "If anything happens to me, Tee, read this. So I'm going to read this poem. For Corrie. *(Pauses. Reads)*

"Do not stand at my grave and weep;
I am not there. I do not sleep.
I am a thousand winds that blow;
I am the diamond glints on snow.
I am the sunlight on ripened grain;
I am the gentle autumn's rain.
When you awaken in the morning's hush,
I am the swift uplifting rush
Of quiet birds in circled flight.
I am the soft star that shines at night.
Do not stand at my grave and cry.
I am not there; I did not die."

VOICE OF CHOIR

Hall – la – lu – jah!

Time: The day of the funeral – that evening.
Place: The Turners' living room.

(The scene opens in the Turners' living room at repass. As the curtain rises and the lights come up, DAVID LEE dressed in a black suit and white shirt sits moodily in a corner, quietly preoccupied with his grief although he is staring at the television set. JONATHAN dressed the same, is at the front door, saying good-bye and thanking a neighbor for coming.)

MRS. BLACKWELL
When your mama wakes up, Jonathan Lee, tell her I'll be back tomorrow morning so we can leave early. If she needs me before then, tell her to just call and I'll come. It's a shame about your sister. God knows it's a shame.

JONATHAN
Thank you Mrs. Blackwell. I'll tell her. Thank you for coming. *(He starts to close door.)*

MRS. BLACKWELL
(Pushing door open for an afterthought) And it's a shame about David Lee, too. Seeing them polka-dot hanging from under those sheets on that stretcher. And, seeing it on television like that. That's too much for a little fellow. Well, let me get on out of here before I lose my grace. Bye, now. **(Exits)**

REV. WILLIAMS
(He has been standing in the background, waiting to say good-bye to JONATHAN) Jonathan, I'm sorry about your sister, Cora Lee. Seventeen is too young an age to die. Such a waste of humanity. She was a fine young lady with so much to offer the

world. But, least we despair, we must try to remember, son, that God works in mysterious ways, his wonders to perform. I'm a witness to that.

JONATHAN

(Weakly) Yeah.

REV. WILLIAMS

Be strong, Jonathan.

JONATHAN

Yeah.

REV. WILLIAMS

Tell your mother I'll see her tomorrow. Good night, now. *(Exits)*

JONATHAN

Good night, Rev. Williams. Thank you. *(JONATHAN closes the door. He leans against the door with his head pressed to the door. He is caught up into his own grief and thoughts. Finally, he turns and begins walking dejectedly toward rear. He notices DAVID LEE, goes over to him looks down at him. DAVID LEE is sitting like a statue, unmoving. JONATHAN passes his hand up and down between DAVID LEE's eyes and the television set. It is obvious DAVID LEE is not seeing the television.)* You watching that, Man?

DAVID LEE

No.

JONATHAN

(He sits beside DAVID LEE, staring blankly at the television. They are both quiet, staring at the set, the volume so low that it cannot be heard) It's been a long day, man. Let's go get some sleep.

DAVID LEE

I'm not sleepy.

JONATHAN

I'm not either, really. But we're probably tired. We just have to make ourselves rest. *(Standing)*

DAVID LEE

Why?

JONATHAN

(Momentarily taken aback) So we can be strong, man.

DAVID LEE

(Angrily) What for?

JONATHAN

(Putting hand on DAVID LEE's shoulder) Whoa, little brother. Hang loose!

DAVID LEE

(Shakes JONATHAN's hand from his shoulder, goes and stands by piano. After a moment he sits at the piano.) I am hanging loose. *(He begins to play CORA LEE's favorite piano piece.)*

JONATHAN

(Sits listening to DAVID LEE play for a few minutes, watching him) I know how you feel, David Lee…

DAVID LEE

I'm Orpheus.

JONATHAN

Huh?

DAVID LEE

That's what she use to call me whenever I played this.

JONATHAN

She did?

DAVID LEE

Uh huh. Orpheus.

JONATHAN

Oh.

DAVID LEE

Who is Orpheus and U – U ....?

JOHNATHAN

And, Eurydice?

DAVID LEE

Yeah.

JONATHAN

Well, in Greek mythology, Orpheus was a fabulous musician and Eurydice was the woman that loved him and loved his music. His music was like yours, man; it charmed anyone that heard it. His music was so out of sight that when the devil heard it, why it enchanted the devil himself.

DAVID LEE

What was Orpheus doing with the devil?

JONATHAN

Well, he had gone to the Underworld looking for Eurydice, see, and...

DAVID LEE

The Underworld? What was Eurydice doing in the Underworld?

JONATHAN

Well..eh.., well, I…I guess you could say – she died.

DAVID LEE

(Stops playing abruptly, turns to look at JONATHAN.) What happened to her?

JONATHAN

(Agitated with subject) She was killed, that's all, and Orpheus went to the Underworld to get her and bring her back home. Hey man, let's stop talking about this Greek shit, anyway.

DAVID LEE

(Quietly) Did he get her?

JONATHAN

(Softly, afraid to answer) No.

DAVID LEE

(Out of control, hitting keys of the piano.) I want her back! I want her back! I want Corrie back!

JONATHAN

(Pulling DAVID LEE to him, trying to comfort him. DAVID LEE refuses to be comforted.) Stop that David Lee, Stop it!

DAVID LEE

(Screaming) I want her back here! I want Corrie! I want Corrie, Jonathan!

JONATHAN

She's gone!

DAVID LEE

(Screaming, out of control.) I want her reincarnated! She said she'd live forever. Forever! She can be born again. She said it. I don't care what she comes back as. She can be anything. I just want her back! I want her reincarnated! She knows how.

JONATHAN

(Near hysteria. JONATHAN grabs DAVID LEE and proceeds to shake him, they are speaking simultaneously.) What are you talking about? Hush, David Lee! You're going to wake up Mama. Hush! Shut up!

DAVID LEE

(Screaming loudly and hysterically) Corrie! Corrie!

JONATHAN

You're going to wake up Mama!

MARGRIT

(Appearing in doorway) Jonathan! Let him be! He has a right to cry. *(DAVID LEE runs to MARGRIT burrows his head into her, crying inaudibly)* You cry, too, son. Nobody can say you haven't got a right to cry.

JONATHAN

(Paces floor, runs hand through hair, trying to compose himself.) David Lee, man, I'm sorry. I...I...Damn! *(Slams hand into fist. Turns back to MARGRIT and DAVID LEE, cries into his hands.)*

MARGRIT
(Moves with DAVID LEE to JONATHAN, embraces both sons)
It's alright, Jonathan.

JONATHAN
(In control) Mama, you shouldn't be up.

MARGRIT
No, I've been resting too long. Come on over here and we'll sit down and talk. *(They all move to sofa)*

JONATHAN
Can I get you something, Mama?

MARGRIT
No, but thank you, anyway. I wasn't sleep – I was just in my room reading my Bible. You know, some people say colored folk put too much stock in the Bible. Maybe we do, but it is a good book. Whenever I've had trouble in the past, I always turned to it and it always helped me. *(Pauses)* You know, today when I stood looking down on my baby's casket, all I could think was, Margrit, you're a stupid woman.

JONATHAN
Mama, don't! Don't blame yourself for what some murdering rednecks did.

MARGRIT
I do blame myself, Jonathan! She tried every way she knew how to tell your Daddy and me that she wasn't safe. But, I was into pretending, Jonathan. I wanted to pretend that we were safe. I wanted to pretend that the law would protect us. I wanted to pretend that things were getting better. *(DAVID LEE has fallen asleep. She stretches his body out on the sofa, then looks around the*

room.) I looked at us and saw a nice house, a car in the garage, piano lessons, children in college, little league baseball and I applied those symbols of middle class status to us. All I could see was progress since we were free of hunger, illiteracy and the sharecropping that my parents suffered from. *(She gets up, goes to piano, softly fingers a few keys)* But I was just pretending, Jonathan, and didn't even know it. Cora Lee tried to tell us nothing important had changed. But, we wouldn't listen. No. We were the grown-up ones and she was just a child, so we wouldn't even listen. *(She is quiet for a while)* I made her go to that church, you know?

JONATHAN
(Protesting) Aw, Mama, don't.

MARGRIT
(Waving him away) Oh, yes I did. I did. Told her she was killing her father. I knew how much she loved that man, so when he had the heart attack, I blamed her. Told her she was killing him by keeping him so upset. I told her that. God! I didn't say a word about the years of discrimination, injustice and oppression. That's what really was killing him. But no, I told her she was killing him because I didn't want her involved in that civil rights mess.

JONATHAN
Mama, you just wanted what was best for her. You were just trying to protect her.

MARGRIT
Yes, but she kept telling me that she was safe nowhere. Nowhere in this country. *(Pauses)* What kind of country is this, Jonathan?

JONATHAN
I don't know, Mama.

MARGRIT

I was stupid enough to think that just because she was sitting in a church, she was safe. *(She is quiet for a moment)* Where is their God, Jonathan?

JONATHAN

Where is ours, Mama?

MARGRIT

Now she's dead and it's my fault. I was hiding behind a wall of pretenses so I couldn't see. Didn't want to see it. But, Cora Lee had, little by little, chipped away until that wall had crumbled and fallen, and she stood face to face with reality. And, that's why she wasn't afraid. She understood that she was no safer sitting in this house than she was sitting in that white public park. She was just as vulnerable in a church as she was sitting in the front of a Jim Crow bus. And, now she's dead and nobody's been arrested and nobody's going to be arrested.

JONATHAN

Maybe they'll catch the son-of-a-bitches! Excuse me mama.

MARGRIT

Don't you start pretending too son. They're not even trying to catch the...the son-of-a-bitches. When we got home from the funeral and I went to my room, I kept thinking how blind I'd been. I just couldn't see around that wall! I felt lower than some snake must feel, down in a black abyss. Here my baby dead and I'm the one sent her to her death.

JONATHAN

(Protesting) Mama.

MARGRIT

So, I got out my Bible and began to read and you know what, Jonathan? It was right there in the Bible all the time. All the time. Isaiah, Chapter II, verse 6. "The wolf also shall dwell with the lamb…and a little child shall lead them." And Cora Lee was that child, trying to lead her scared, meek sheep of parents to better grounds. Away from that wolf cloaked in white skin and calling itself human. And, all over the South, these children – these children have been the ones, refusing to accept what we old folk were pretending to be progress. They've been leading us just as the Bible prophesied. When I look back, Jonathan, I realize that I was willing to accept being a lesser human being because that was easier than fighting back. But, tomorrow… *(The telephone rings, interrupting her and startling DAVID LEE out of sleep. JONATHAN goes to answer it.)*

JONATHAN

Hello? Dad! Are you O.K.? *(Brief silence)* No, she's not sleep. We were just sitting here talking. Here she is Dad. Hurry and get well. O.K. Bye. *(Hands phone to MARGRIT.)*

MARGRIT

(Into Phone) Franklin! Are you O.K.? Honey, honey it just couldn't be helped. Don't worry about missing it. The doctors said that you just were not strong enough to get out of bed today. It's probably for the best, anyway. It's best you remember her the way she was. O.K. Alright. *(Long pause)* Yes, I'm still here. Franklin, in all the years we've been married, I've never kept a secret from you. You know that, don't you, honey? I know this isn't a good time to upset you, but you have a right to know. *(Pauses)* Tomorrow, there's going to be a … I guess you'd call it a wade-in at the public beach. For the first time in my life, Franklin,… I'm going to the beach! *(She is so overcome with emotion that she begins to cry.)* This is 1955, this is America, and I am going to the

beach! *(She begins to laugh heartily. She turns away from the phone and speak to her sons.)* He says he's noticed lately that I could stand a good sun-tan. *(Speaking into the phone again)* Yes he's right here. Now? *(To DAVID LEE)* David Lee, your father says go get his knotty pine box and bring it to me. *(DAVID LEE exits to rear. MARGRIT speaks into the phone again)* I'm going to take off my shoes, Franklin, and walk into that warm sand, right up to the water's edge. Then I'm going to step into that beautiful blue water as if God made it just for me. All hell can break loose on this earth, but I'm going into that water tomorrow! *(DAVID LEE returns with box, gives it to MARGRIT. She opens it, takes out something. She speaks again into the phone.)* Yes, Franklin, I have the hundred dollar bill. *(She turns to JONATHAN and speaks.)* He told me to give this to you, Jonathan. He says use it to bail me out of jail tomorrow.

JONATHAN

(EXITED) Let me talk to him. Dad, I need a suntan myself, man, so I won't be able to bail her out. I'll need someone to bail me out, too! O.K. Dad. Thank you *(He gives the phone to DAVID LEE)* He wants me to talk to you, man.

DAVID LEE

Hi, Daddy! Yes, I'm O.K. You O.K.? *(Pause)* They won't let me bail them out of jail, Daddy. I'm just a little kid, you know that. Anyway, I'm going to the beach too, so I'll be in jail, Daddy. *(Pauses)* Naw, I'm not going to be scared. I'm a little kid, but I'm not no baby! *(Pause)* He says give the money to Mrs. Blackwell and ask her to bail us out, Mama.

MARGRIT

Tell him Mrs. Blackwell asked if she could ride to the beach with me.

DAVID LEE

(Speaking into phone.) Mama says Mrs. Blackwell is going to the beach, too. I bet she's going to still be kicking! *(Laughs. He imitates FRANKLIN.)* Daddy said, I'll just have to get up out this bed and come bail y'all out my own self! *(They all laugh.)* O.K., Daddy, Bye. *(DAVID LEE hangs up telephone.)*

MARGRIT

Knowing your Daddy, he'll do just that.

JONATHAN

I know he will, Mama. I know he will. *(They exit with MARGRIT embracing JONATHAN and DAVID LEE)*

(The lights dim. Spotlights go to television. All this time, the television has been on with the volume low. As the characters walk through rear door, the volume on the television increases. We hear the television announcer. Time has passed; eight years. As the announcer begins to speak, a huge screen begins to drop slowly from the ceiling. It show the masses at the March on Washington. The screen is showing what is supposedly on the television.)

VOICE OF TELEVISION ANNOUNCER

Today is August 28, 1963. This is an historic day in the annals of this country. Millions, I repeat, millions of people are marching on Washington. There are black, white, and people of every color and description. There are old people in wheelchairs and babies in arms. There are nuns and priests and rabbis, walking arm-in-arm with Baptist ministers. There are Northerners and Southerners and Americans from all over the country. Area airports, train and bus stations are literally packed with thousands flowing into this capital hourly. America has come today, marching into this nation's capital in the name of freedom and justice for all Americans. It is, indeed, a great day in this country's history. Never have so many gathered in one place to make one statement. As our camera sweeps down from the stairs of the Lincoln Monument, we see that the people are countless and as the camera sweeps further away, we see that they're still coming and coming and coming and coming and coming.... *(The announcer's voice dims. Superimposed on his voice, we begin to hear the unmistakable voice of CORA LEE. She is speaking to JONATHAN at the party, telling her philosophy of the one-ness of mankind. In the background, we faintly hear the music of her favorite song. We sharply and clearly hear her speaking voice as we see the March on Washington.)*

CORA LEE'S VOICE

"But when I woke up that morning in jail, it came to me that We is all of us, Jon. It's all the people in this country. Not just Negroes, and not just whites either. It's all the people in the world. We! We! And the vast majority of people are good. I know that now. And there has to be millions of people on our side – on the side of right – on the side of good – on the side of justice. Millions, Jon. And they are coming! And when I saw it, I was so happy, I started to cry."

CURTAIN

THE END

129

EPILOGUE

Nonviolent resistance... is based on the conviction that the universe is on the side of justice. Consequently, the believer in nonviolence has deep faith in the future. This faith is another reason why the nonviolent resister can accept suffering without retaliation. For he knows that in his struggle for justice he has cosmic companionship.

Martin Luther King, Jr.

WORKS BY
LORETTA A. HAWKINS

My Cousin, Juju—May 2017

Of Quiet Birds—September 2017

The Way We Be—September 2017

Dese Shoes and Other Poems—September 2017

Published by FIREKEEPER ARTISTRY
Chicago, Illinois